INTERVIEWING

Glynis M. Breakwell

Problems in Practice

This series is the natural successor to the popular *Psychology in Action* series, and continues and extends the aim of 'giving psychology away', that is, making psychological expertise more freely available.

Each title focuses on a common problem across a number of different professions – industry, education, medicine, the police and other public and social services. The approach is practical, drawing on examples from a range of work situations. And the reader is constantly invited to look at problems both as object and subject: accepting help as well as offering help; both giving and requesting expert advice. Psychologists have a great deal to say about how to improve our working lives and the aim here is to offer both practical skills and new insights.

THE AUTHORS AND EDITORS
Glynis Breakwell (Reader in Psychology, University of Surrey, Guildford)
David Fontana (Reader in Educational Psychology, University of Wales College of Cardiff)
Glenys Parry (Regional Tutor in Clinical Psychology, Knowle Hospital, Fareham and Top Grade Clinical Psychologist, Department of Psychotherapy, Royal South Hants Hospital, Southampton)

The original, problem-solving approach of this series was applied also to the creation of these titles, by a team of three, acting as both authors and editors. Each member of the team, drawing on their own practical experience, contributed ideas, material and criticism to every title, in addition to taking full responsibility for the writing of one or more of them. This approach ensures a book of wide practical relevance, combining the strengths and expertise of all authors, a uniformity of approach with a minimum of overlap between titles, yet retaining the clear, simple line of the single-authored book. The commitment of the authors to the series made all of this possible.

OTHER TITLES IN THE SERIES
Managing Stress by David Fontana
Facing Physical Violence by Glynis Breakwell
Coping with Crises by Glenys Parry
Social Skills at Work by David Fontana

Problems in Practice

INTERVIEWING

Glynis M. Breakwell

Reader in Psychology
University of Surrey

Published by The British Psychological Society
and Routledge Ltd.

To Chris Fife-Schaw

First published in 1990 by The British Psychological Society, St Andrews
House, 48 Princess Road East, Leicester, LE1 7DR, in association with
Routledge Ltd, 11 New Fetter Lane, London EC4P 4EE, and in the USA by
Routledge, Chapman & Hall Inc., 29 West 35th Street, New York NY 10001.

British Library Cataloguing in Publication Data
Breakwell, Glynis
    Interviewing. – (Problems in practice series)
    1. Interviewing
    I. Title II. Series
    158'.3

    ISBN 1–85433–001–2

Library of Congress Cataloging-in-Publication Data is available.

Printed in Great Britain by BPCC Wheatons Ltd, Exeter

Contents

INTRODUCTION TO THE SERIES   ii
FOREWORD   vii

1. WHAT IS INTERVIEWING?

Interviewing and professional practice   2
Types of interview   3
    Selection interviews – Appraisal interviews –
    Research interviews – Media interviews
The ethics of interviewing   8

Exercise 1: WHAT INTERVIEWING DO YOU DO? *4–5*

2. INFORMAL INTERVIEWS

Planning: the employer's perspective   10
Planning: the applicant's perspective   17
Head hunting   20

Box 1: PROS & CONS OF INFORMAL INTERVIEWS *12–13*
Exercise 2: DECIDING WHETHER TO APPLY *21*

3. ONE-TO-ONE SELECTION INTERVIEWS

Six tasks for the interviewer   23
Biases in the selection process   27
Conducting the interview   35
Interviewee strategies   45

Exercise 3: YOUR IDEAL CANDIDATE *25*
Box 3: THE IDEAL INTERVIEWEE *32–33*
Box 4: PSYCHOMETRIC TESTING *38*
Box 5: STANDARD TRAPS FOR INTERVIEWERS *40–41*

4. SELECTION PANELS & GROUP INTERVIEWS

Organising the panel   51
Chairing a panel interview   53
Panel interviews: the candidate's perspective   54
Group interviews   55
Validity and reliability of selection interview assessments   58

5. APPRAISAL INTERVIEWS

The purpose of appraisal interviews   61
How to prepare yourself for appraisal   63
Acting as an appraiser   66
Choosing an appraiser   69

Exercise 4: APPRAISING YOURSELF 65
Exercise 5: APPRAISAL FEEDBACK 67

6. RESEARCH INTERVIEWS

Action research and programme evaluation   70
Designing research   71
Analysing information from research interviews   83
Presentation of findings   89

Exercise 6: CALCULATING A RESPONSE RATE 74
Box 6: GROUP INTERVIEWS: PROS & CONS 75
Box 7: GROUP INTERVIEWS: DOS & DON'TS 76–77
Exercise 7: CREATE AN INTERVIEW SCHEDULE 82
Box 8: TELEPHONE INTERVIEWING 84
Exercise 8: REPORTING FINDINGS 88

7. INTERVIEWS WITH CHILDREN

Hazards in interviewing children   90

8. MEDIA INTERVIEWS

Making the best of an interview   95
Taking an active part   100
Exercise 9: MAKE A MEDIA MESSAGE 96
Exercise 10: MEDIA INTERVIEWS BY TELEPHONE 99

REFERENCES   100
FURTHER READING   100

Index   102

Foreword

Interviews form an important part of working life for all professionals. Although professionals may be trained in specific techniques of interviewing clients or members of the public (think, for example, of the police, doctors or social workers), we are rarely expert in the kind of interviews that are common across all types of work.

Selection interviews, staff appraisal, research interviewing, talking to the press – many people launch into these activities, whether as interviewer or interviewee, without a clear understanding of what they are doing. The results can be dismal. With the benefit of hindsight we might realise our mistake – entirely the wrong person has been appointed to the job, the research information gained is incomplete, the newspaper article puts across a misleading picture – with the help of quotes from our interview! Perhaps most disappointing of all is not getting the job one wants because of an interview that goes badly. In each of these examples a valuable opportunity has been missed.

Yet interviews have been extensively researched by psychologists and much is known about human behaviour in interviews. Glynis Breakwell makes this psychological knowledge available and accessible to all of us in a way that is immediately useful. For example, Dr Breakwell shows that we often have false assumptions about the interview process and she wittily demonstrates the ways that we can allow biases to affect the outcome. She then shows how to make selection interviews a more valid and reliable way of predicting the individual's later performance. There is invaluable help here too for anyone thinking of applying for a new job – deciding if the new job is worth applying for, and making the very best of one's chances during informal and formal appraisal.

In each type of interview, psychological insights are applied constructively to produce a more effective encounter, for both parties. Even experienced interviewers will find much that is new and useful here.

Glenys Parry and David Fontana
Series Editors

Chapter One

What Is Interviewing?

WHAT IS AN INTERVIEW?

There is more to being a good interviewer than asking the questions you want to have answered. There is more to being a successful interviewee than answering the questions that you are asked. This book describes how to conduct interviews from both perspectives: that of the interviewer and that of the interviewee. It shows how both should prepare for an interview, what they need to do during the interview, and how they can later make sense of what happened in it. This dual emphasis on interviewer and interviewee is needed because neither can understand what to do without knowing something of what the other is trying to do. Dealing with an interview effectively requires that you see what is happening from the other's point of view as well as your own. If nothing else, this helps you to predict what might happen next. The dual emphasis is also needed because the same person can change from being an interviewer at one time or in one context to being an interviewee at another time or another place. The manager who is on the selection panel for a job today may be being interviewed for another tomorrow.

Interviewing is used for many different purposes. It is tempting when thinking about interviewing to focus solely upon job interviews but interviewing is used in many other contexts – anywhere, in fact, where people wish to get and give information in an orderly fashion. In an interview, there are always rules which govern the flow of that information, determining who can ask what, of whom, and when, as well as the shape that answers can take. According to the type of interview, the rules differ in specificity and formality. The main purpose of this book is to describe the skills needed to operate according to the rules in various sorts of interview: those used in recruitment, in staff appraisal, in research, and in the media.

INTERVIEWING AND PROFESSIONAL PRACTICE

Interviewing is central to the activity of most educationalists, health care professionals and social and public service personnel, and many managers in industry and commerce. Sometimes this is formally acknowledged and training in interviewing techniques is incorporated into courses leading to professional qualifications. Often interviewing is an integral part of tasks identified with specific professional groups: diagnosis in medicine, compiling case histories in social work, producing nursing records in nursing, counselling in psychology, staff guidance in personnel work and interrogation in police work. Interviewing is part of the professional role of all practitioners because they rely upon being able to elicit accurate information from the people with whom they work. Each profession focuses upon different techniques of interviewing depending upon its responsibilities and legal powers.

Practitioners with any experience normally become very skilled in the interviewing techniques directly necessary to their professional activities with the public. The problems arise when they step into a different context. Increasingly, they can expect to be involved in a range of activities; almost everyone at some stage becomes involved in some form of management. This may involve staff recruitment and selection. It may also involve staff appraisal or assessment. Many have to conduct evaluations of the services they provide; assessing the effectiveness of their own work and that of others. Some find themselves either defending or promoting the work they do through the press, radio or TV. Each of these additional roles is likely to involve interviewing. In some cases the practitioner is the interviewer; in others, the interviewee.

The techniques of interviewing required in these various contexts differ. Selection and appraisal interviewing have some things in common but they also differ significantly from each other and from research or media interviews. They all differ from the standard professional interview with someone who needs help. So, for instance, a head teacher interviewing a child to establish why he has a black eye, truants and never has lunch money would need to use a different technique from those she uses when interviewing a council planner to establish why her budget for the new science block has been sliced or interviewing a candidate for the job as head of the maths department. Similarly, the hospital administrator would need to employ different tactics when interviewing a nursing sister who has inexplicably tendered her resignation than when interviewing contractors who wish to do the laundry.

As practitioners move into new contexts and take up different roles requiring management and research skills, it is important for them to acquire new interviewing techniques appropriate to the new context and the role. It is counterproductive to rely upon techniques effective in other contexts. Of course, it is not easy to drop interviewing habits built upon earlier professional experience. Sometimes they infiltrate so unobtrusively that you only know that it has happened when you look back. One of the major objectives of this book is to outline appropriate interviewing styles for the broader range of activities required in professional practice. Practitioners can then consciously choose which tactics to use in each situation.

Before continuing with this chapter, please complete Exercise 1. Such exercises appear throughout the book. They serve three purposes:

1. *To encourage self-assessment.* They ask you to reflect on your current goals, skills and problems; they, therefore, allow you to focus more clearly on those aspects of your interviewing activities which should be changed.

2. *To uncover stereotypes and misconceptions.* Interviewing is fraught with all sorts of biases; these exercises help you to identify what biases affect you and other people you have to deal with.

3. *To try out the methods and skills outlined in the book.* These exercises provide a testing ground for you to practise some of the techniques described.

In some places in the book, Boxes are used to summarise key information or strategies which should be remembered when dealing with interviews. These Boxes are designed to provide quick reminders of essential points that you can refer to before embarking on any interview.

TYPES OF INTERVIEW

This book explores four very important types of interview:

- selection interviews
- appraisal interviews
- research interviews
- media interviews

WHAT INTERVIEWING DO YOU DO?

EXERCISE 1

The object of this Exercise is to get you to think about your own previous experiences of interviewing and to encourage you to analyse what additional skills you need to acquire.

1. List all the types of interviewing in which you have been involved whether as an interviewer or as an interviewee.

2. Rate how well you think you generally perform in each type of interview situation listed (as interviewer and interviewee separately). A rating of 5 = 'very well', 4 = 'quite well', 3 = 'uncertain', 2 = 'quite badly', and 1 = 'very badly'.

INTERVIEW SITUATIONS   PERFORMANCE RATING

● *As an interviewer*   *(Scale 1 – 5)*

1.

2.

3.

● *As an interviewee*

4.

5.

6.

3. Consider those features of each type of interview which you find particularly difficult and make a list of them. Be specific – these difficulties can become targets for change. Focus in turn upon each phase of the interview: the preparation, the actual interview and the period just after the interview. Try to describe for yourself the problems you experience both as an interviewer and an interviewee in each phase of the interview.

PARTICULAR DIFFICULTIES

● *Pre-interview*

  1.

  2.

● *Interview*

  1.

  2.

● *Post-interview*

  1.

  2.

Use your list to decide whether different types of interview involve different types of difficulty for you. How do you usually handle the difficulties? Can methods for coping with difficulties in one type of interview be used in others?

4. What information do you need to have in order to improve your performance? Make a list of what you see to be the key questions you want answered. You may wish to use this list to target which information to look for in the rest of the book.

5. What training have you had in interviewing techniques? Have you been able to put that training into practice? If not, list what obstacles you have experienced. Again, the list should be used when reading the book to estimate what resistance you might experience in using the methods recommended. Estimate the likely opposition, you can then work out strategies for overcoming it.

SELECTION INTERVIEWS

Both informal and formal interviews in the context of selection will be considered. 'Informal interviews' are occurring more frequently now in professional practice. They occur prior to the formal job interview and offer the applicant a chance to discuss the job and see the work environment often before making a final decision to apply for the job. They also offer the prospective employer (and sometimes prospective colleagues) the opportunity to influence what the applicant thinks of the job and may indirectly shape the shortlist for formal interview by dissuading marginal candidates from carrying on with the application. The informal interview is open to considerable misuse and can be an occasion for misinformation. Some techniques for self-protection in informal interviews are suggested in Chapter 2.

Formal selection interviews now encompass a range of methods: they can involve one interviewer or several in a panel; they can involve an individual or a group of interviewees; they can entail a sequence of exchanges, sometimes spread over some days; and they can be used in tandem with other assessment techniques, such as psychometric tests. Each type of selection interview requires somewhat different tactics. Chapter 3 indicates prime features of the one-to-one selection interview. Chapter 4 considers panel interviews and group interviews.

It is worth emphasising that selection interviewing is not just about asking questions; to do it well you need to know how to use the answers. Chapters 3 and 4 also show how to structure questions so that the answers they elicit are usable.

APPRAISAL INTERVIEWS

Most professions have moved towards some variant of 'management by objectives', and some are now using very sophisticated assessment and review procedures far removed from the naive, narrowly-specified, task-oriented early approaches. The basic method typically entails establishing performance indicators for each type of job. The success of each person is then measured against how far he or she achieves clearly specified objectives within a given timescale. Inherent in this approach is the need for regular appraisal. Chapter 5 examines how interviewing fits into the framework of appraisal and evaluation against performance indicators. Clearly, interviewing can be used to elicit information about performance but it also plays a central role in the negotiation of indicators and objectives.

Both appraisers and those being appraised need to know how to use the interview optimally. This includes understanding the peculiarities of repeat interviews, perhaps taking place at annual intervals over several years, where they involve co-workers. It touches upon the features to look for in choosing an appraiser, the training needed for appraisal, and the anxiety of being an appraiser. It emphasises that appraisal can be an opportunity rather than a hurdle. It can be, on both sides, a legitimate time-out for planning and re-orientation.

RESEARCH INTERVIEWS

In some professions, research has always been assumed to be part of the role. For instance, doctors and nurses have often expected to contribute to research monitoring the impact of new treatments by reporting what their patients say about side-effects. Similarly, social workers have frequently become involved in evaluating the effects on clients of introducing different rules in residential settings such as old people's homes or hostels for young people. But now other practitioners are finding it necessary too. There is now a growing emphasis upon practitioners conducting their own action research or evaluation programmes. These are designed mainly to assess the impact of changes in practice or the organisation of the services provided. Middle-level practitioners (with some management or budgetary control) often want to know whether small-scale, local changes are effective either in terms of cost or of service delivery. They often use interviews (formal and informal) to collect feedback from their staff or the public. For instance, head teachers, with the advent of parent governors and other similar changes, are finding it increasingly important to check that their schools are providing the service wanted in their communities. This may mean establishing that the range of courses offered is adequate: it may mean finding out if the school buildings are being used optimally outside school hours. Testing the opinion of the community, especially its most influential members, can become important in planning the role of the school. This may not be labelled 'research' by the teachers doing it but, in fact, it is.

This trend might be expected to grow stronger as moves towards management by objective and performance indicators require proof of 'value' before new resources are released. This will push more practitioners to look for methods of assessing service provision. The caring professions rarely employ researchers from outside. They tend to be too costly and too ignorant of the way the profession works to gain easy entry. In-house small-scale research is the order of the day; unfortunately, most practitioners are not trained in the social research methods needed. The basic principles for conducting research interviews and for interpreting the results are described in Chapter 6. They include advice on how to present results to others effectively: organisational issues, use of summaries, providing clear substantiation of conclusions which avoid over-statement, and describing carefully the origin of the data used.

MEDIA INTERVIEWS

The media are ever more present in the lives of all professionals whether they work in the public services, industry or commerce. They call for justification and explanation of the performance and powers of the professions. Chapter 8 looks at techniques for dealing with aggressive or antipathetic media interviewers as well as dealing with the sympathetic. It explores the differences between passive and active interactions with the media. Most often, someone from the media will approach you for information. Sometimes you may wish to approach the media; for instance, if you want to advertise a service or promote a cause or enlist the public's help. Where the exchange is in your interests, your tactics will differ from those where the interview is motivated by the interests of the media.

THE ETHICS OF INTERVIEWING

It is important when dealing with each type of interview never to lose sight of the ethics of the situation. There are three major issues to consider.

1. *How do you ask questions about sensitive issues?* This really revolves around the rights and responsibilities of the interviewer. Do you have the right to ask certain questions because they are relevant to decisions you need to make even if they concern areas of the person's life that are very private? For instance, in a selection interview, should you ask whether the applicant has a settled family background? Or, in the appraisal interview, should you try to check out your suspicion that over-indulgence in alcohol explains poor performance? Deciding how far to go is no easy matter. Throughout the book, this issue is examined against specific examples.

2. *What do you do if you unearth an unresolved problem incidentally?* It is

necessary to be prepared for the unexpected when interviewing. For instance, a research interview conducted to establish whether a local drop-in centre is providing the right facilities might be used, by the interviewee, as a chance to unload major fears about the impotence he has experienced ever since he was made redundant. What do you do in this situation? There is a temptation to offer direct advice or intervene based on your own professional experience. This may be inadvisable. Some of the pitfalls surrounding these sorts of unexpected disclosure will be described at various points in the book.

3. *What feedback do you give after the interview?* Too often no feedback is given to interviewees. Mostly, this failure is a product of laziness, poor organisation, or simple lack of concern. In most contexts there is no real excuse for failure to give feedback. It may be difficult and embarrassing to have to tell someone what they did badly in the interview, but it is still a responsibility which the interviewer has. The ways in which feedback can be given constructively are presented in the book.

Some of these ethical issues become acute when dealing with some sectors of the community. Chapter 7 is devoted to the special difficulties involved in interviewing children; consideration of them is used to heighten awareness of how interviewing tactics must always take account of the capacity, status and knowledge of the interviewee.

WHAT DO YOU NEED TO KNOW ABOUT INTERVIEWING?

The book is based on the assumption that you need to know about:

❑ being both interviewer and interviewee – in one-to-one, panel and group interviews;

❑ interviewing techniques in the context of selection, appraisal, and evaluation research – this includes understanding something of each phase involved: preparation, interaction, information recording and analysis, and feedback;

❑ the special difficulties of dealing with some sorts of interviewee (for example, children);

❑ being interviewed by the media;

❑ the ethical issues embedded in the interviewing process.

Chapter Two

Informal Interviews

When looking for a new job or looking for new staff it is important to decide whether you want to become involved in informal interviewing before the formal selection interview. The pros and cons of informal interviewing are summarised for the prospective applicant and the employer in Box 1. There is a trend towards informal interviewing now in most professions. Sometimes informal interviews are arranged without thinking about what purpose they might serve. They have become part of the done thing. It is worth stepping back from habits and standard procedures and making a conscious decision about their value in each individual case. Once you decide to become involved, this chapter should help you to do everything in your power to maximise the advantages and minimise the impact of the disadvantages.

PLANNING: THE EMPLOYER'S PERSPECTIVE

Know the objectives of the interview

Informal interviews often degenerate into entertaining but pointless chitchat unless the interviewer has a hit list of topics to cover worked out before the prospective applicant arrives. This hit list should include:

(a) What you want to tell the applicant about the job and the employing organisation. One of the main reasons for conducting an informal interview is to 'sell' the job to the applicant. If you are desperate for staff, as many public service employers now are, especially in the high income

regions, the informal interview can be a vital time for selling yourself. In determining what information you give you should remember that:

☐ The applicant probably has the same professional preoccupations as yourself but it is sensible to confirm this before launching into great detail on a single aspect of the job. As a general rule, it is unproductive to make assumptions about the knowledge or attitudes of the interviewee.

☐ Information is best given hierarchically: give the overall picture first and then fill in the details. You should remember that, even in an informal interview, the applicant is likely to be nervous and this impairs the ability to memorise and recall information. It is, therefore, valuable to have the main points you need to get across on paper ready to hand out. This would be in addition to the job and organisational descriptions sent out to all potential applications prior to the informal interview. (Duplication of information can be off-putting.)

You should also note that people have a limited span of attention. They are more likely to remember information given in small spurts (lasting about 7–12 minutes) which encourage interaction than that given in long monologues. In any one information-giving session, they might be expected to assimilate seven new simple pieces of information. If the information is complex or interconnected (as it probably will be) they can absorb less (normally about four themes or arguments). Again, this suggests that aides-mémoires should be provided early in the interview.

☐ Give the balanced picture of the job; too rosy a picture will smell suspicious. The balance you should aim for would show the disadvantages of the job but would range them against the backdrop of larger advantages. The same balance should be struck in describing the wider employing organisation. There are major ethical questions that arise if information on the drawbacks associated with the job is incomplete. The employer will be the only one with the full details of the job and to fail to provide central details, perhaps because the applicant fails to ask about them, is not acceptable. It is also foolhardy in the long-term, since an applicant who is ill-informed on starting the job will operate less effectively and, once the real drawbacks become apparent, may choose to leave. Honesty may reduce the field of applicants but it makes practical as well as ethical sense.

(b) What you want to show the applicant. Working environment is an important determiner of satisfaction in a job. Most people coming for

PROS AND CONS OF INFORMAL INTERVIEWS

FOR THE EMPLOYER

BOX 1

Pros

1. Provides an opportunity to 'sell' the job and the employing organisation by emphasising the hidden, non-obvious advantages of the post.

2. Publicises the work of the organisation to a group of potential future employees.

3. Involves a broad range of colleagues in vetting applicants.

4. Provides additional information on which to base further pruning of the shortlist.

5. Gives encouraging feedback to good applicants.

6. Allows applicants to disabuse themselves of misconceptions about the job and, possibly, self-select out.

Cons

1. Interviewing can be time-consuming.

2. Requires careful prior preparation of programme, information hand-outs and appropriate questions.

3. May reveal more about the job and work environment, including work colleagues, than you would like.

4. Lays you open to awkward questions which are normally silenced by the formality of the selection interview.

5. Relies upon existing staff cooperating and not sabotaging the event by allowing their prejudices to show either with regard to the applicants or the job.

FOR THE APPLICANT

Pros

1. Provides useful insights into the work environment and prospective colleagues. It may also allow you to glimpse future patients/clients/pupils.

2. You can ask more questions in greater detail than would be expected in the selection interview.

3. Allows you to work out what isues should be pursued at the formal interview.

4. Provides some idea of what the level of your opposition or competition is like.

5. Gives you the chance to gauge what type of person they want to fill the job.

Cons

1. Information provided by the prospective employer or colleagues can be misleading or overstated, especially when given as an informal aside.

2. The informality of the interview can be disarming and result in you becoming too relaxed and too willing to disclose information about yourself.

3. No clear criteria for the successful conduct of an informal interview are normally given. This may mean that you do not know what should be your goals in this context. Preparation is difficult. Self-assessment of performance in retrospect is equally problematic.

4. Prejudices can be expressed relatively untrammelled by legal restraints in an informal interview. Exposure to them may make you unsure of yourself and, perhaps, unwilling to pursue the application.

an informal interview will want to see where they would work and get a feel for the resources and support available. If you are keen to persuade someone that the job is attractive, it may be vital to show the positive aspects of the working environment.

The work environment undoubtedly includes the characteristics of colleagues. Consequently, it is important to choose who else will talk to the applicant very carefully. It is generally a mistake to have more than two other people talk to them. The more people they speak to, the more repetitious the information and the more diffuse the impact. They may even get contradictory messages. It is therefore advisable to brief staff who take part in informal interviewing. Each participant should know more or less what area of information must be covered and in what order and by whom. Setting up a clear programme for the period when the applicant visits also makes it less likely that there will be confusion about where he or she should go next.

(c) What you want to ask the applicant. You should make a point of asking the applicant who has not yet decided whether to put in an application form before the informal interview to supply some background information in advance (maybe in the form of a c.v.). If you do not have some information prior to the interview, you will spend too much time piecing together the picture of their qualifications and work experience, especially with older applicants. Since the major battery of selection questions will be asked later in the formal interview, the informal interview should be used mainly to clarify information given by the applicant about background and work history. The objective is to identify any hidden or omitted information which might be pertinent to the shortlisting exercise. For instance, it is important to check out any gaps in the education or work history. You might want to confirm medical information. You might need to assess whether there are any factors which would make it unlikely that the job would be accepted if offered.

You must also decide how questions will be asked. The guidelines for asking answerable and informative questions are described in Chapter 3. All the techniques described there can be applied in informal interviewing.

TIMETABLE INFORMAL INTERVIEWING CAREFULLY

You are likely to have several people to interview; therefore, you need to decide whether they should all be seen during the same day or not. If they are, should they be given opportunities to talk to each other?

Seeing everyone in a condensed time period has advantages: briefings can be done in groups; comparisons between applicants can be made with memories of all of them fresh; if several other staff are involved it facilitates coordination of their activities; and so on.

Allowing applicants to talk to each other has drawbacks. They will inevitably engage in comparisons amongst themselves. In some cases, this will mean that the less confident pull out because they feel the field is too strong. In other cases, it will mean that the strong pull out because they feel that the inferior quality of the other applicants indicates that the job would not be sufficiently demanding or rewarding. Since there seem to be few advantages in allowing applicants to meet at the informal interview stage, it is probably best avoided.

The informal interviews need to take place sufficiently in advance of the formal selection interview to make it possible for late applicants to be added to the shortlist or for someone who clearly has no chance of appointment to be removed. To have informal interviews after the shortlist has been declared is nonsensical.

SYSTEMATISE THE RECORDING OF INFORMATION

Where several people are seeing an applicant sequentially in an informal interview, it often happens that information they elicit is either not systematically recorded or is not subsequently pooled. This detracts from the value of the exercise considerably. If the suggestion that all interviewers have a clear idea of the programme for the recruitment session is followed, it is possible to give each of them a way of recording the information they collect.

At its simplest, this might mean giving them a list of questions they should cover without fail and a piece of paper for each applicant (with the names of the applicant and the interviewer) on which they record the information together with any additional comments they might have. These record sheets can then be used at a session where interviewers pool their responses to each applicant and share the information they have gathered. The record sheets would then also be available for those involved in the formal selection interviews. Since the informal and selection interviews may involve quite different interviewers, this continuity in the recording of information may be important. The standard record allows others to use it later and minimises opportunities for idiosyncratic biases in reporting information.

The use of the record sheet which includes the list of questions has another advantage. Having to cover a particular range of questions may mitigate interviewer discrimination or biases. The nature of interviewer bias is fully covered in the next chapter. Suffice it to say here that the informal interview can be just as subject to discriminatory practices as the selection interview. In fact, in some ways discrimination has freer reign because in the formal selection interview there are normative and legal constraints which do not operate so well in the informal interview. Informally, someone might be more likely to ask something which can be construed as sexist, racist or ageist.

Of course, this will not eliminate other ways in which discrimination can slip into the interview. The other major channel of bias operates through the interpretation of information. Even where the same questions are posed to all applicants, their responses will be open to selective recording and differential weighting directed by prejudice. There is no simple way to overcome this problem. Some methods are discussed in the next chapter.

GIVE FEEDBACK

If an applicant is not shortlisted after the informal interview, feedback on shortcomings and suggested modifications in approach or preparation may be valued. Obviously, this may be too time-demanding and not feasible; however, if the applicant might be a likely candidate for some other post in the future, there are advantages in making the rejection more palatable and, perhaps, including an outline of upcoming jobs. It may also be worthwhile giving constructive feedback if the applicant comes from a community of practitioners that you regularly wish to tap. Applicants share their experiences of interviews with colleagues. Negative reports from one applicant can dissuade others from applying to you in the future.

Of course, you may also wish to give feedback to good applicants in order to encourage them to attend the selection interview and not drop out. It can be tempting to make informal job offers or something that looks like a promise of the job before the selection interview. This is normally inadvisable since, besides being unethical, it may mean the favoured applicant fails to perform so well on the day of the selection interview because there is no charge provided by uncertainty. Your co-interviewers might then find your preference inexplicable. It is also possible that other applicants will show greater strengths under the pressure of the formal interview. Curtailing your options prematurely often leads to regret.

IS AN INFORMAL INTERVIEW NECESSARY?

You may decide that an informal interview round is superfluous. There is then a difficulty if applicants expect to be able to come to talk 'informally'.

Since the practice is definitely the norm in many professional settings, the applicant may think you have something to hide or are not serious about the advertisement (perhaps because you prefer a strong internal applicant). It may be necessary to offer informal interviews to avoid such suspicions.

If you decide to do this, it is important to offer the same opportunities to all applicants. Sometimes informal interviews are provided only for those who specifically request them. This can lead to considerable disparities of knowledge about the job and the organisation on the part of applicants by the time they get to the selection interview. It can seriously disadvantage those who did not understand that an informal interview was available. To ensure equal opportunities, all applicants should be informed that they can have an informal interview if one is offered to anybody.

PLANNING: THE APPLICANT'S PERSPECTIVE

There are parallels between the perspectives of the employer and the applicant on planning informal interviews. The applicant must:

DECIDE WHAT INFORMATION YOU NEED TO GET

Prepare a list of questions that the employer needs to answer. This will doubtless have to cover questions not answered in the job description about the nature of the work. It may also cover questions not normally touched upon in a job description such as promotion prospects, opportunities for further training, rates of turnover of personnel in this level of job, extent of flexibility in the salary on offer, and so on. If it is of concern to you, questions about the likelihood of management changes in the employing organisation could be asked too.

In addition, you should ask a series of questions which allow you to create a fairly firm profile of the type of person they want for the job. These questions can be direct: for instance, you can ask what qualifications are required for the job, what minimum level of experience is expected, and what specific skills are called for in the job. You can also use indirect questions: what sort of person would best fit into the current staff group, what was the previous job occupant like and do they want the new person to be similar, or what qualities does someone need in order to work effectively with the client/patient/student group concerned?

DO YOU FIT THE JOB?

Having established the profile of the person that they want, you need to decide how closely it fits you. If the fit is not too good, you must decide whether you would be able, or indeed wish, to change to get closer to it.

Of course, alternatively, you can attempt to persuade them to alter the profile. This may be feasible to some extent during the informal interview. You can attempt to show them that the qualities necessary for the job differ somewhat from those they had anticipated. Obviously, this has to be done carefully. Interviewers are alert to the fact that you are motivated solely by self-interest. One tactic would be to describe how the same functions are performed by someone with different experience in other organisations which you know. Ask them if the person appointed really needs as much experience of nursing that particular speciality as they had expected; you know of other hospitals where the transition occurs quicker. Describe how, in your present school, staff effectively cover subsidiary subjects, if needed, without prior experience of teaching them. Another tactic might be to query the practical relevance of some central trait in the profile. If you do challenge the profile directly you need to do it in a very detailed fashion with concrete examples of what you find unconvincing about their ideal. If they want someone with a particular educational background, for instance, and you do not have it, you might need to explain that the job does not require certain formal qualifications; that practical experience has provided you with similar skills. You would then have to describe these skills clearly, showing that someone with the education they initially wanted would not possess different or better skills.

In many cases, changing the profile may only be possible from within, once you have the job. This might mean shaping the profile of yourself (your personality, aspects of your past experience, future aspirations, or expectations about workstyles) which you present at selection interview to fit that required. Some of your characteristics would be brought to the fore in your self-presentation; others would be omitted or diminished. Once you have the job, the object would then be to change what is expected of someone in that job, over time, through example. With the exception of certain core components, most aspects of a job description will be rewritten by the incumbent.

MAXIMISE YOUR INFORMATION ABOUT THE ORGANISATION AND THE JOB

Most interviewers are disproportionately impressed if you show that you have 'done your homework'. You may not get all the details right but you show that you are serious about wanting the job. Getting the background right will also ward against gross naivety in your questions.

CALCULATE THE STRENGTHS AND WEAKNESSES OF YOUR COMPETITORS

This may be useful in helping you to decide which aspects of your skills or experience to emphasise when it comes to the selection interview. You can focus upon those features which make you appear more fitted for the job.

The assessment of the opposition may also help later in negotiating salary if you are offered the job. If you are the outstanding candidate, the only one of those shortlisted they really want to work for them, you should be ready to take advantage of it. Even in those professions where there are nationally-agreed salary scales, there is normally some flexibility at the margin. The starting point on the scale, the level of removal expenses, help with the mortgage, the engine capacity of any lease or company car provided, and so on, can all enter into the negotiation to make the job a more attractive proposition for you. The point at which they offer you the job is the time to push this negotiation but the informal interview is the time to work out what you can ask for.

AVOID EXCESSIVE SELF-DISCLOSURE

Prior to going, you should decide what sort of information about yourself and your attitude to the job you wish to disclose during the informal interview. The informality of the event tends to lull people into a false sense of security. It is certainly inadvisable to get into a long explanation of why you wish to leave a current job. Any explanation of the move should be short and unrevealing of any difficulties you have had in the job. Expressions of boredom with the work or serious conflict with the management in your current job should be avoided. Focus instead upon your enthusiasm for the job on offer, on the challenges it provides and the career prospects you see in it. Appear to be running towards something rather than away from something.

Generally, interviewers will want to know why you are applying for the job. You need to know this yourself, of course. The reasons you give yourself may be complex, interconnected and, to the outsider, even confused or mutually exclusive. The reasons that you give the interviewer need bear no resemblance to those you give yourself. The ones you make public must be clear, logically-related and immediately understood. This separation of the personal and public explanations for decisions is difficult to handle. It can be particularly difficult for members of the education and caring professions who are often trained to give priority to their own thoughts and feelings. Some of the tension which this generates can be dispelled if, in constructing the public explanation, you present authentic reasons but simplify them.

dissipé

RECORD WHAT YOU LEARNT IN THE INFORMAL INTERVIEW

This can have two purposes. First, it may be some time before the selection interview occurs and recall of information is imperfect at the best of times. When anxious, you will memorise things less effectively. Take notes during the interview if need be. If not, make them immediately after the event. Second, constructing the record will allow you to organise and interpret the significance of information more easily. You can then decide whether you want to persist in your application. The informal interview should be treated seriously as a filter point in the application process. If you do not like what you see, you should pull out. You may even choose to explain to the employer why you have decided to do so. This feedback to the employer may be useful. Interviewers normally have surprisingly little feedback on their performance.

Much of what has been said about informal interviewing serves to highlight that it is the overture to the selection interview. Many techniques transfer between the two. Some of the suggestions which follow in Chapters 3 and 4 could be implemented just as well at the stage of informal interviewing.

HEAD HUNTING

Everything that has been said about informal interviewing assumes that the staff involved are average employees. There are occasions when an organisation has to go out its way to attract specific people. This may be because they are known to be 'high flyers' in their field and have a track record of outstanding success. In the public services, this might apply to some specialists or to senior management personnel. It is now recognised that organisations will 'head hunt' individuals whom they particularly need. They may even employ a head-hunting company to do the negotiations for them.

Clearly, in head hunting the power balance in the negotiations has shifted. Typically in informal interviewing, the power lies largely with

— DECIDING WHETHER TO APPLY —

EXERCISE 2

Some features of a job are listed below. First, rank them in order of importance to you personally. Next, rate your current job on each of them. Then, rate the job that you are considering applying for. Ratings should be done on a five-point scale:

5 = the feature is present in the job to a large extent
4 = the feature is present in the job but not very much
3 = uncertain whether the feature applies to the job
2 = the feature is definitely not present in the job
1 = the feature could never be present in the job

Rank in importance	Job Features	current job	prospective job
	Good salary		
	Good use of your abilities and expertise		
	Good physical work environment		
	Reasonable travel to work time		
	Good colleagues		
	Real opportunities to help other people		
	Job security		
	Good hours of work		
	Offers prestige/status		
	Fits your overall career plan		
	Offers power to make and execute decisions		
	Good ethos/good management in the organisation		
	Training/chances for skill development		
	Promotion possibilities		
	Interesting client group		
	Does not interfere with family life		

Add other features applicable to your type of work.

Once you have completed the ratings, compare the scores. Is the prospective job scoring higher on those features which you consider more important? If it does, it is probably worth going for it. Obviously, the decision also needs to take account of those features where it fails to score as highly as your current job. Do they matter to you? These are purely personal decisions. There are no rules of thumb which can be applied generally. The checklist is designed to help you organise your evaluations of the two jobs systematically. It cannot tell you what to do.

the employing organisation; it decides who to employ, when to take them on, and what work they should do. In head hunting, the power is very much in the hands of the individual whom the organisation needs. This means that preliminary interviews with the organisation, or its agents, can be structured by the individual who will have an agenda of objectives that have to be met. Many of the considerations which are covered in this chapter would nevertheless apply in preparing for such preliminary interviews. However, the candidate might be more at liberty to require additional information from the organisation prior to the informal interview. For instance, details of how the post became vacant, long-term development plans in the organisation, assurances of promotion or incentive deals, and so on. In this situation, the informal interview is the venue for negotiation of employment terms rather than assessment of the candidate.

Chapter Three

One-to-One Selection Interviews

There are many forms of selection interviewing. The focus in this chapter will be upon general features and principles of selection interviews, with especial reference to one-to-one interviewing. The next chapter deals with panel and group interviews.

SIX TASKS FOR THE INTERVIEWER

Interviewer Task 1. Conduct a job analysis. The first task for someone wanting to make a job appointment is to conduct a job analysis. This entails breaking the job down into its constituent parts: what role must the occupant perform, and what tasks must be done? Next, the relative importance of each of these job components should be determined. If you have never done a job analysis, it might be informative to do this for your own job. It can sometimes be illuminating because you may be doing many things which you do not consider to be a legitimate part of your role.

The second part of job analysis requires you to establish what qualifications, expertise and experience anyone would need in order to do the job effectively. It is legitimate at this stage to identify any personal qualities that would be essential if the person appointed is to function optimally in the organisation. Your shopping list of characteristics might then encompass calmness in the face of stubborn, irascible superiors, the capacity to tolerate boredom, flexibility about hours worked, and so on.

Interviewer Task 2. Write a job description. The job description will include an outline of those features of the job, and the applicant, which have emerged from the job analysis. There may be some applicant characteristics which you would not wish to include in the job description (for example, calmness in opposition to management) because they are too difficult to articulate and may even sound silly. But, as a general rule, the job description should be as full and precise as you can make it. In the long run, this saves time since unsuitable people will recognise that there is no point in applying.

Interviewer Task 3. Advertise. It is important in advertising a vacancy to choose the right media. Every professional group has its own trade rags and these are obvious targets. But the quality daily newspapers can also widen the range of potential applicants. For jobs which are likely to be attractive to people already in the area, local radio can be very effective. The thing to watch for is any unintended bias in the pool of potential applicants introduced by your choice of advertising medium. Some media will only reach a small part of your pool; supplement these with others. Of course, in producing the advertisement, you need to be very clear about the job description and it is vital to avoid unwittingly including any cues or triggers which will act in a discriminatory way. For instance, in advertising the job of a part-time care assistant in a residential hostel, it would imply that a woman was preferred if you pointed out that the hours would suit someone who had to collect children from school.

Interviewer Task 4. List the essential selection criteria. You need to extrapolate from the job analysis what essential criteria an applicant must satisfy in order to be shortlisted and you should be able to articulate these criteria unambiguously. For instance, if experience is important in the job, you should be able to specify what type of experience, over what period, with whom, and so on.

Once you have a clear list of criteria these can be used to generate the questions included in the application form. This may mean that standard application forms need to be supplemented by additional sheets. In structuring the questions on the application form, every effort should be made to encourage quantifiable answers. You want to know not just whether they have a particular type of experience, but how much they have. This list of criteria will also help you to ask specific questions of referees. The problem with using referees' comments is that they are often either irrelevant or they are non-comparable across applicants. In asking for referees' reports, it is permissible to detail those aspects of the applicant that you want them to comment on.

YOUR IDEAL CANDIDATE

EXERCISE 3

▶ Take a job you know well and think it would be good to have but not your own. Perhaps you could use one for which you have recently been involved in recruiting. List all of the characteristics which you would expect the ideal candidate for that job to have. The list will cover qualifications and experience but it should also focus upon personal qualities: intellectual level, personality traits, leisure interests, etc.

▶ Next rate yourself on each of these qualities. Be as honest as you can. Rate 5 if you possess the quality to a great extent, 4 = quite a lot, 3 = uncertain, 2 = not much, and 1 = not at all. For those qualities where you find that you score 5, ask yourself whether this quality is really necessary for the job concerned. Would you include this quality if it were not something you believe is typical of yourself? Make explicit your reasons for including each quality. Are they strong or weak reasons?

When setting up the personal profiles required for a job it is always instructive to go through this Exercise. It highlights biases which may be entering into the selection criteria that you establish.

Interviewer Task 5. Weight the selection criteria. Decide on the relative importance of the selection criteria. One way of doing this is to allocate points out of a total of 100; the more important get more points. The schema might look like this:

Relevant past experience	20 points
Proven capacity to adapt and learn	20 points
Management skills	10 points
Able to bring new skills	5 points
Would work well with people with whom we work	10 points
Communication skills	10 points
Enthusiasm	5 points
Personality attributes	20 points

Of course, your own list will be more detailed and specific. Once you have decided the relative weights, you can then rate each applicant against each criterion out of the number of points allocated to that criterion. So, for instance, one candidate might get 4 out of 5 for 'enthusiasm' and 10 out of 20 for 'relevant past experience'. If the scores are then summed across all criteria the final total incorporates the relative importance allotted to each criterion. The applicant with the highest score should then be offered the job.

Things are rarely that simple, however. Sticking to the scoring system often proves difficult. The results may not always match your intuitive response to applicants, especially when some characteristic is manifest in the interview, which you had not anticipated, and which swamps all other considerations (either positively or negatively). For instance, you may discover that the prime candidate on all the established criteria has a heart condition which might be incapacitating at any time. A problem then arises since you have not asked other candidates about their health. What weight then should you place upon your doubts about the health of this prime candidate?

Interviewer Task 6. Determine the interview structure. You may not be able to use all of the selection criteria at the shortlisting stage because it may be impossible to tap some types of information (for example, data on 'enthusiasm') through the applicant's self report, though it may be feasible to do so by using referees' comments. By the time you get to interview you should have translated the criteria into a series of tasks which allow applicants to show how far they can satisfy the criteria.

Traditionally, interviews have involved direct questions. You want to know about a person's experience, so you ask them directly about it. You want to know if they like working with children, the old, pregnant women, etc., and you ask them. Increasingly, the selection process now incorporates other ways of getting information. Psychometric tests of personality, aptitudes, and ability are used. Analysis of handwriting is employed regularly, especially in the USA, even though it has been shown in recent studies to be an unreliable means of assessing character. Group discussions, game playing, role enactment and planning exercises are all quite popular. Some of these techniques are considered in Chapter 4. For the moment, the point to be made is that you need to decide which type of task will best expose particular characteristics.

The traditional form of one-to-one direct questioning is best used to collect factual information (including chasing up omissions or disinformation in the application form about background), to address issues which might be sensitive or embarrassing, to assess formal communication skills, and to assess technical knowledge.

BIASES IN THE SELECTION PROCESS

Before going on to discuss techniques which should be remembered when using direct questioning methods, it is worth looking at biases which enter into the selection process.

IMAGES OF THE IDEAL CANDIDATE

Figure 2 depicts the stages in the selection process at which images of the ideal candidate come into play. Both the organisation and the possible applicant hold images of the ideal occupant of the job on offer. The ideal exists at two levels: the generic and the specific.

At the *generic* level the organisation has an image of the ideal member of staff. Typically such an image has four main components.

- 1. PEDIGREE
- 2. PRODUCTIVITY
- 3. PROSPECTS
- 4. PERSONAL SKILLS

PEDIGREE refers to having been educated and trained at a good institution (whether college, university, hospital or institute) and having worked previously with members of the profession who have high status.

PRODUCTIVITY can be defined in many ways. It might entail proven administrative skill, the ability to handle heavy workloads, evidence of good time management, or previous success in introducing organisational change. With the move towards the 'enterprise culture' in the caring and education professions, productivity will probably come to encompass earning power: people who attract money or investment into the organisation will be valuable producers.

PROSPECTS covers the general sense that this person is going places. Organisations benefit from the subsequent success of employees, including past employees. The organisation in making an appointment, especially one involving the dedication of training resources, is taking a gamble and making an investment. It wants to believe that the person will win for it. This will include, of course, being able to change with it.

PERSONAL SKILLS would be seen to include leadership potential, ability to work well with others, and general communication skills.

The 'ideal' has all four Ps. Indeed, a fifth P may be added: PERFECTION. This may sound silly but it creeps insidiously into discussions about applicants for jobs. Interviewers are heard to say:

'But does she have that little bit extra?'

'He's shown no real flashes of alpha.'

'None of them are quite as good as applicants used to be.'

The important point about the generic ideal is that it forms the backdrop to decisions in the specific case. There are no absolute or objective indices which can be said to measure the five Ps. This means that they become part of the rhetoric of job selection; they allow infinite room for manoeuvre. If an interviewer dislikes a candidate, there is always the *Prospects Ploy* to use. This would involve questions like: 'Do we really think that this person can grow as the job demands increase?' The beauty of it is that no one knows. The spanner is well and truly launched into the works because the shadow of doubt is cast over that applicant. Doubt, no matter how inconsequential, can stall an interview panel which was moving torwards a decision. Doubt can be equally well generated using the other Ps.

Personal Skills Scam: 'I can't really see this one being able to handle a violent client at midnight in an emergency ward, can you?'

Productivity Protest: 'Well, I can see that he's been very productive in the past but the last year or so have been a disappointment – bad sign for the future?'

Pedigree Query: 'I've seen people from that place in the past – not very reliable you know.'

And, of course, the *Perfection Smear:* 'Doesn't seem to have IT to me.' (IT should never be specified, if you use this tactic.)

The generic ideal created by an organisation will directly and indirectly influence the prospective applicant's image of someone acceptable as a member of staff. The generic ideal will permeate all dealings the applicant has with the organisation. It will focus emphasis in briefing sessions, illustrate advertising material, shine through the structure of questions posed on application forms, and so on.

Increasingly, organisations in which the public service professions work are heavily committed to corporate and institutional image building. The corporate image which portrays the ethos of the organisation (whether it is a hospital, local education authority or social service department) is likely to have the generic ideal of staff embedded in it. To the extent that the corporate image is established, it will add weight to the messages about what is required of staff, which an applicant receives.

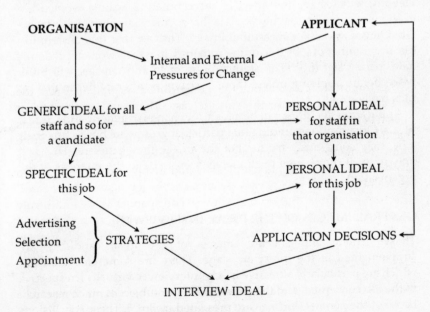

Figure 2: Stages in selection where bias can occur

Obviously, the generic ideal appears in a somewhat different guise for each specific job, incorporating the qualities unique to that job. This specific ideal then directs advertising, selection and appointment strategies.

A prospective applicant will form an image of the specific ideal for someone doing the job based on the generic ideal already created and on the details of the advertising, selection and appointment strategies adopted. Prospective applicants compare themselves with their image of the ideal occupant of the job, and if they believe that they do not match up to this, they are unlikely to pursue their application.

This means that the image of the ideal candidate promulgated by the organisation, through its recruitment strategies or possibly through its efforts at corporate image building, can act as a sieve, filtering out some applicants. If the sieve is being used deliberately, this may not matter but often filtering is unintended, with bias creeping in unnoticed. For instance, a requisite of the job description might be that the appointee should be energetic. The translation of this during the recruitment process might entail descriptors like 'active', 'vigorous', or 'enthusiastic'. The word 'youthful' may not be uttered but it starts to look strange that it is not there. The cues trigger a youth stereotype. There may have been no intention to discourage older applicants but this is the actual upshot.

Stories of hidden agendas in advertising and in recruitment interviewing which have the effect of discriminating against women are even more common. Saying a job is 'hard', 'dirty' and 'involves unsociable hours' gives it a masculine image. The fact that this description fits any number of jobs (including nursing), in which women predominate, barely signifies. The stereotype is male and females will think twice before applying unless there is strong counter-evidence that no bias really exists.

Application decisions can be a force for change in generic and specific ideals. Organisations, finding that particular groups are boycotting their jobs, may consciously try to alter the image they generate. This will only occur if the change is ultimately seen to be in the interests of the organisation.

GENERAL IMAGES OF THE IDEAL INTERVIEWEE

These generic and specific images of the ideal candidate are supplemented at the interview stage. There are some characteristics which are particularly attractive in any interviewee virtually irrespective of the job concerned, and these have been the subject of much research. Some of the general findings are presented in Box 3. These conclusions are based on a diverse array of research methods. Some have involved observations of real interviews; others use responses which are elicited to descriptions of hypothetical interviews. Some have used strictly controlled experiments; others have relied upon large-scale surveys. As a consequence, the statistical approaches have differed ranging from simple comparisons of frequency distributions to rather elaborate path analyses. Only the implications of these studies are presented in Box 3. (Further information is available in Smith and Robertson, 1989; Glick et al. 1988; and Orpen, 1984.)

Box 3 summarises a set of generalisations which mask considerable individual differences. This does not detract from the importance of the biases. Interviewers and interviewees alike should be aware that these biases exist and are manifested often enough to make it likely that everyone will encounter them at some point. As an interviewer, knowing about them could make you less likely to succumb to them. As an interviewee, knowing about them may enable you to play upon them deliberately.

INTERVIEWER DIFFERENCES IN TYPES OF BIAS

Some work has been done on differences between interviewers in biases. It seems that female interviewers are more likely to appoint attractive applicants (irrespective of their sex). Female interviewers value honesty and openness in an applicant to a greater extent than do male interviewers. They also prefer women applicants who are non-traditional in their views and aspirations more than men do. Female interviewers are more likely to look for enthusiasm to be shown by the applicant. This is echoed in female applicants who try to show greater levels of enthusiasm. Male interviewers are less interested in the leisure activities of applicants and less likely to discuss their ambitions. Male applicants are less willing to talk about their non-work life, especially to a male interviewer. Male interviewers are less willing to express disagreement with an applicant. Female interviewers are more likely to show humour during the interview. Female interviewees feel less able to bluff a female interviewer. This may partially explain why female–female applicant–interviewer pairings produce greater openness on the part of the applicant. Male pairs go the opposite way. Clearly, you ignore the sex of the interviewer at your peril.

One other strange but interesting finding is that interviewers who are very concerned to monitor their own performance and the effect that they are having upon others tend to emphasise the importance of physical attractiveness when making appointments. There is some

THE IDEAL INTERVIEWEE

BOX 3

❏ **Application form is tidy,** with all the questions answered and whatever space allowed for each is used completely. (The exception to this occurs in the computing profession where scruffy application forms with extra sheets of information added are deemed better!)

❏ **Answers questions** at interview; does not ask more than the minimum.

❏ **Is physically attractive** (as defined by cultural norms). Physical attractiveness is particularly important where the job is sex-typed (traditionally associated with one sex) and the applicant is of the other sex. Physical attractiveness is influential in hiring decisions for males in both managerial and clerical jobs, but only for clerical or administrative jobs for females.

❏ **Shows moderate levels of aggression** during the interview. There is actually some doubt as to whether the studies which show this are really monitoring aggression or simply assertiveness. Certainly, a confident, assured presentation of one's abilities and views is effective for most types of job interview. Failure to illustrate that you can look after yourself when challenged in the interview is disadvantageous.

❏ **Is similar to the interviewer.** This similarity can be at a number of levels: age, sex, education, past employment, expressed attitudes or values, even speech patterns. This process can explain sometimes how discrimination operates against certain groups: they are less successful at interview because they are dissimilar from those who interview them. This may be because they are female and the interviewers are male or they are black and the interviewers are white, and so on. Interviewers tend to be drawn from powerful groups within our society. It is not surprising then that the pressure to prefer people similar to oneself perpetuates existing power differentials and bolsters institutionalised discrimination.

❏ **Demographic characteristics** (age, sex, race, etc.) operate indirectly. Studies of the demographic characteristics of applicants show that they have their effect upon hiring decisions by changing perceptions of the applicant's skill, intelligence and likeability. For instance, interviewers who find than an applicant's demographic profile does not match what they want tend to rationalise their rejection by downgrading estimates of the skill, intelligence or likeability of the applicant. When these estimates, at least of skill and intelligence, are compared with objective indices, this bias is evident.

❏ **Is tied into prestige networks.** Applicants who have influential contacts, even if these are irrelevant to the job itself, have a greater chance of being hired.

❏ **Dresses appropriately.** In most professional contexts, potency (strength and constancy) is associated with dark clothing. Acceptability for senior management posts seems to be tied to the presentation of a 'masculine' image in clothes. This applies to female applicants too. Considerable research has been done to establish what constitutes 'masculine' dress for a woman which will be effective without going over the top. Masculine features include dark colours, strong angular lines, large-scale details, straight silhouettes, and heavy textures. Female applicants get higher ratings if they incorporate some (but not all) of these features into their garb.

❏ **Sex-typing of jobs** makes the interviewee ideal gender-specific. In jobs which are stereotypically-associated with men, female applicants are evaluated on different criteria to their male counterparts. They need to be better qualified and they should manifest the 'masculine' personality traits most associated with the job in question. The target traits will differ across jobs but might include: abrasiveness, lack of emotionality, using relationships for ulterior motives, etc. It is notable that women of high ability who apply for sex-typed jobs may be over-valued by interviewers. It seems that when she applies for a 'male job', a woman is expected to lack the requisite characteristics; when the interviewer finds this preconception is erroneous in a particular case, the woman achieves high credibility.

suggestion that this is because they know that an attractive co-worker will increase their own kudos in the eyes of other people. As an interviewer, if you find you are considering the physical attractions of a candidate, it is always best to question your own motives.

USING WHAT YOU KNOW ABOUT SELECTION BIASES

It should be possible to use what is known about selection biases to improve the fairness of recruitment practices. Greater fairness could be achieved if:

● Organisations and their interviewers encouraged the explicit articulation of ideal images (whether at the generic, specific or interviewee levels). This would include some attempt to show how the ideal is translated into the objective criteria against which individuals are judged. For instance, if the ideal candidate has 7–10 years' experience in the profession, an extrovert personality, and a genuine concern for doing a good job, the employer should be able to say so. While the length of experience is easily translated into an objective criterion, personality and concern are more difficult, but indicators can be chosen (for example, level of involvement in social activities or leisure preferences, or even responses to psychological tests for personality). Shifts in the way this translation occurs which introduce discrimination would then be visible. People could not get away with the prospects ploy, personal skills scam, productivity protest, pedigree query or the perfection smear.

● Organisations should train their selection interviewers about the biases which enter at all levels of the selection process: from job analysis, through advertising strategies to the interview questions. In large organisations there may be room for a watch-dog empowered to check out what has happened in any appointment. Personnel departments rarely fulfil this function.

● Prospective candidates should be made aware of the ideals which underpin criteria as well as the criteria themselves. This will allow people to make appropriate decisions about applying. This approach would dispel the myths which grow up around particular organisations. Everyone will recognise such myths: 'It's no use applying for a job at that school, they only ever take Oxbridge graduates'; 'That social work team would never appoint a man'; 'That community practice wants entrepreneurs and administrators not doctors'; and so on.

Finally, in considering selection biases, it is worth remembering that the same fundamental biases influence promotion decisions.

CONDUCTING THE INTERVIEW

During a selection interview the interviewer has a very complex set of tasks to accomplish:

▶ applicants must be set at ease so as to facilitate their optimum performance

▶ directly relevant information must be collected

▶ information must be recorded in some way so that it can be used at the point when a decision is made

▶ judgements need to be made about the validity of the information given by the applicant

▶ applicants' questions must be answered clearly.

There are some guidelines for executing these tasks.

SETTING APPLICANTS AT EASE

Try to arrange for candidates to get to the venue of the interview in good time so that they can be given coffee/tea before you start. Giving candidates drinks during the interview can fluster them.

On entering the interview room, make clear introductions to everyone present; preferably explain why each is there. If there are several interviewers involved, it can help immensely for the applicant to be given a seating plan (name and function of seat occupant included). Remember: anxiety impairs memory; ensure that the candidate has an aid to memory for any information which is central to the interview.

Some people favour beginning with routine social chat such as 'Was your trip here okay?'. This is unnecessary and may distract the candidate (especially if their trip included some untoward event). It is probably better to start with a simple description of the job. This should already be familiar to the candidate and will be easy to absorb and reassuring. This can be followed up with introductory questions which are non-threatening: asking them to rehearse their qualifications and experience, for instance. At this point it is as well to get over the stock questions which they will have been expecting you to ask: for instance, 'Why do you want this job?'; 'Why do you want to leave your current employ-

ment?'; 'What do you think you can bring to this job which is special?'
Avoid using jargon or mannered expressions in your questions. This
should apply throughout but particularly at the start.

If it is genuine, positive feedback on performance at this stage of the
interview (and indeed later) will help to put the candidate at ease.
Remember that you want to see all that the candidate has to offer.
Anything which makes them present themselves fully (including warts)
is useful. Saying that you recognise that they have thought an issue
through, or that their answer has been persuasive, can help. This will
lay the right foundation for moving on to the next stage of the interview
where you may wish to be quite challenging.

ELICITING RELEVANT INFORMATION

Know the purpose of the question you are asking. If it is designed to
tap the level of professional knowledge on a particular topic make sure
that (*a*) it does not incorporate extraneous issues, and (*b*) you are aware
of the full range of possible correct answers.

It helps if questions are presented directly and one at a time. Do not
preface a question with a long opinionated preamble. The connections
between a series of questions may be unclear to the candidate even
though they are obvious to you. If a number of questions are linked
by a common theme which needs to be taken into account by the
interviewee, tell them so.

TESTING ANALYTICAL ABILITY

You will probably want to evaluate the candidate's ability to analyse
the pros and cons of an issue or course of action. Sometimes, hypothetical
scenarios are used to do this: for instance, the candidate is told a story
about a relevant event which happened to some mythical person and
they are expected to say what they would have done. Thus, a candidate
for a teaching post which involves handling classes which are racially
mixed might be asked to say what he or she would have done if faced
with a racially-motivated fight in the classroom. Such scenarios can be
a way of addressing very complex issues. They work well with candidates who are used to operating in the 'if this, then that' realm of formal
reasoning. For those who find imagining themselves into situations
difficult, they do not work so well and it is better to use concrete
examples. So, for instance, you might ask them whether they had ever
experienced the type of event that interests you or whether they knew
of such an event. Having created the concrete image for them, it is

then possible to go on to ask how they reacted or would expect to react. In both cases, you can ask for a balanced analysis of the most appropriate course of action.

Changing the way in which you pose questions that are designed to tap analytical ability relies upon your sensitivity to the experience, style and ability of the candidate. You need to be alert to misunderstandings which may be a product of differences between yourself and the candidate in style, experience or background. Differences in ways of talking (accent, dialect, and vocabulary) and types of non-verbal communication (posture, willingness to get close to someone else, and eye contact) between the interviewer and the candidate can cause confusions. Both tend to interpret what the other says or does in terms of the standards expected by their own age or ethnic group, class and gender. Where one might see the avoidance of eye contact as an expression of insolence, the other might experience it as courtesy.

ASKING SENSITIVE QUESTIONS

The selection criteria may require that you ask sensitive questions which touch upon personal matters. These might include drinking habits, marital relations, medical history, domestic arrangements, and so on. First, you have to decide if these questions are really necessary. The criterion should be: would I appoint someone irrespective of this information? Second, you should establish if a question is legal. For instance, questions about a spouse's attitude to the candidate taking the job, child care arrangements, etc., are only legally permissible if they are asked of all candidates irrespective of sex. If sensitive questions are necessary and legal, two precautions help.

● Acknowledge that you recognise that the question is personal and may be offensive or distressing and, if this is the case, say that the candidate does not have to answer.

● Explain why the answer is important in the selection procedure (having to do this will ensure that you have to convince yourself that it really is necessary).

Having gone through these precautions, you should then ask the question in a direct and forthright way. Do not beat about the bush. This only accentuates embarrassment for you and the candidate. Rehearsal of the question is consequently advisable, and it is preferable to use a standard wording for it.

PSYCHOMETRIC TESTING

BOX 4

'A test is a systematic procedure for observing behaviour and describing it with the aid of numerical scales or fixed categories' (Cronbach, 1984, p.26)

Over the last 80 years, psychologists have developed tests to measure all kinds of personal characteristics: physical and intellectual abilities, aptitudes, and attitudes. There are now thousands of psychometric tests. Most are listed in a regular publication, *The Mental Measurement Yearbook* (Buros Institute for Mental Measurement, University of Nebraska). Tests vary in form: they may be paper-and-pencil exercises, they may involve actual manipulation of small objects, and sometimes involve extensive physical activity. Psychometric tests are standardised in the sense that the tester's administration, scoring and interpretation of the test are fixed so that scores from different people, at different times or places can be meaningfully compared. To be accepted, tests must be validated: that is, they must have been shown to measure the quality they are said to measure. They must also be reliable: that is, the score for any one individual must be reproducible over time.

In the majority of cases, the correct administration of the test and interpretation of results is not simple. Before using most tests it is necessary to go through a careful training. Tests are, therefore, not readily available to the general public. Publishers and copyright holders often place restrictions on their sale. In some cases, users are required to attain a certain proficiency in administering and interpreting the test by attending appropriate training courses before being allowed to purchase the test. In others, test developers have retained control over the intepretation of test scores offering a service to those who use the test.

Psychometric tests which are properly validated and standardised are very effective tools for the assessment of ability and personality and can be used to predict subsequent performance. They should, however, be used only by someone appropriately trained in their administration and interpretation. If you want to use a psychometric test in your selection procedure, make sure you are properly trained to do so or call in an expert to do it for you. If in doubt about your qualification to use it, check with the publisher, distributor or the test developer.

ASSESSING PERSONALITY

Personality traits are usually an important part of selection criteria. It is unfortunately the case that interviewers are notoriously bad at assessing personality. This is hardly surprising given the short period of interaction involved in most interviews and the biases which we know to be at work. If you really do need reliable estimates of personality, it is safer to supplement interview information with psychometric testing. Reputable personality questionnaires, administered and analysed by professional psychologists, can be very informative. They are normally more reliable than assessments made in one-to-one interviews.

In asking questions there are standard traps into which most interviews fall. These are summarised in Box 5. It is best to avoid them if you can.

RECORDING INFORMATION

Never rely on your memory for what the candidate has said during the interview. Memory is creative: it elaborates to suit prejudices. Memory is selective: it censors the unexpected or the unacceptable.

You should take pre-structured notes of the key information. Prepare your questions in advance and leave a space next to each where notes can be made. Since note-taking can be intrusive in a one-to-one interview, you should explain to the candidate the reason why you are doing it. In fact they may be reassured by your unwillingness to trust to memory where their future is concerned. The intrusion of note-taking can be minimised if you use a keyword system, which involves having some idea in advance of the types of response a question will elicit and giving each a number or keyword. When a candidate produces one of your stock replies, you just enter the number or keyword. If you are interested in the extent to which the candidate evinces particular qualities or knowledge, the keyword system can be complemented by a 5-point rating system. First, you note what response is given, then you rate the degree of intensity with which it is produced. For example, you might be interested in the difficulties the candidate would envisage when working with a particular client. Let us say that you were appointing for a social work job and the client group concerned were the residents at a geriatric hostel. You might expect the answers would cover the physical handicaps of the clients, their psychological state, their interaction with each other, the lack of adequate staffing, and so on. Each type of difficulty is given a keyword. The rating would then reflect how important the candidate thought each difficulty was (i.e. how far it was stressed in the answer).

STANDARD TRAPS FOR INTERVIEWERS

BOX 5

1. **Failing to concentrate upon the other person:** worrying about what the candidate thinks of you and trying to make a good impression at the cost of getting the information needed.

2. **Failing to notice candidates' difficulties:** slight hearing deficits, problems with understanding your accent, problems arising from cultural differences between you (for example, sub-cultural linguistic differences).

3. **Introducing irrelevances:** reminiscences, giving personal examples, pursuing something the candidate says because it is personally relevant to you, and so on. Self-disclosure should be restrained. The note to hit is *friendly, interested neutrality*.

4. **Indicating boredom** or impatience: rifling through papers on your desk; interrupting too quickly; not answering questions adequately.

5. **Failing to be consistent** in the pattern of questions asked across candidates so that the information collected is not comparable.

6. **Talking too much:** allowing the candidate no real space to think about an answer; if there is a pause, you jump in to fill the verbal vacuum. This can be a symptom of anxiety, or it can be your habitual style. Try counting to 20 before pursuing a question if you feel an impending attack of verbosity.

7. **Making instant global evaluations** of whether you like a candidate. Some people seem to glory in making snap decisions about candidates which they will never change. This is sheer self-aggrandisement, normally based upon the delusion that they are good judges of character.

8. **Ignoring the selection criteria** and following 'instinct', 'intuition' or 'feelings'. This is accompanied by a tendency to use rating on one or two non-central criteria as justification. For example, the argument might go: 'We want someone with interests outside of work and this chap is the local rugby club's captain – that also proves he has leadership ability.'

9. **Using leading questions.** The expected answer is implied in the way you ask a question. For example, you might ask: 'I suppose you would never cope with the situation in that way?' What could the candidate say but 'No'. The ability of a question to predispose the answer need not be a matter of the actual words. It can be in the delivery: tone of voice, inflection, hesitation.

10. **Failing to arrange the best physical environment** for the interview. Confrontations across large desks provide a poor venue for self-disclosure. Chairs set near a table at a 45 degree angle encourage relaxed interaction as long as they not too close to each other.

11. **Losing control of the interview.** This most frequently happens with a candidate who blathers – rambling from one topic to another without pause and often without any obvious connecting thought. There are many reasons why candidates do this. Anxiety: they talk so as not to hear the silence when they stop. Fear: they may fear your questions and if they carry on talking it reduces your opportunity to pose difficult ones. Loquacious nonsense can also be a product of the desire to please. The candidate does not know quite what answer you want so gives you everything. A direct intervention which points out that you were looking for a short but lucid answer should suffice to control the flow. You can also lose the initiative to the candidate who interrupts your questions. This can be addressed by shortening the questions but sticking to your theme. The same tactic can be used with the candidate who becomes confused and answers tangentially.

JUDGING THE VALIDITY OF INFORMATION GIVEN

This is actually a major problem. Candidates are quite sophisticated in interview technique nowadays. They know the conventional pattern of questioning and they know the conventional answers to give. They know that you should never admit to disliking your current job. They know that you should claim to be seeking a new job to provide new challenges and to follow a career plan. One way to break into this cycle of predictability is to respond to the conventional answer with scepticism. Let candidates know that you recognise the conventional answer and ask why they think everyone gives that answer. In their response, you should be looking for the willingness to go beyond the convention, to add the flavour of idiosyncrasy and uniqueness. You should also be looking for discrepancies in the answers given. Pointing out discrepancies can be used as another sort of challenge to provoke clearer self-presentation.

Clearly, in making these challenges, you need to monitor the candidate's reaction. The challenge should be done with good humour; it should not appear like an attack. If it is interpreted as an attack, the interview can rapidly descend into a vortex of monosyllabic answers.

MONITORING NON-VERBAL COMMUNICATION

Pay close attention to the non-verbal communication pattern of the candidate in order to assess both the impact of your questions and the likely truthfulness of the answers. Non-verbal communication (NVC) covers all behaviour, other than that which is verbal, which carries some meaning. So it would include bodily posture (normally a good index of relaxation), respiration rate and sweating (indicators of anxiety), eye contact (a cue to turn-taking in conversation), and so on. The problem with using NVC in an interview as an indicator of what a person is thinking or feeling is that it is subject to too many idiosyncrasies. For one person, stillness might mean calm acceptance, in another it might mean fright. Maintaining eye contact could mean an attempt at deception or truthfulness. If you are dealing with someone over a period of time, you can learn their NVC style and come to interpret it reasonably reliably. This is not feasible in an interview. The most you can expect from NVC cues in an interview is an indication of when a change in mood has occurred. You would still have a hard time finding out what the direction of the change was. Nevertheless, NVC should not be ignored. NVC is more difficult to counterfeit than language. Lying with words is easier than lying with NVC because facial expressions which convey emotion cannot be controlled as easily as the words which describe those emotions. This means that it is useful when discussing a candidate's emotional responses to particular events to watch for the NVC accompaniment.

USING REFEREES' REPORTS

There are, of course, indirect routes to verification of information given in the interview. It can be done by using application form answers or referees' reports. Referees' reports are tricky sources of information. Referees selected by the candidate are unlikely to provide overtly negative information about them. However, conscience and professional obligation may well lead them to build in a subtext to the reference where criticisms are implied by omissions or caveats. Referees' reports should therefore be read for what they do not say as well as for what they do. Ask yourself, what feature which is central to this job does the referee not mention? Then ask the candidate about it.

ANSWERING CANDIDATES' QUESTIONS CLEARLY

This may seem obvious. However, there is a considerable body of evidence which shows that candidates leave interviews feeling that their questions have not been answered; or, they subsequently find that the answers given were false.

Candidates get misinformation mainly because interviewers dislike losing the edge in an interview by admitting that they do not know the answer to a question. The best strategy is to acknowledge your ignorance and offer to find out the answer as soon as you can. If you make this promise it is important to keep it. The psychological impact of failure to honour promises made at an interview can be considerable, especially if the candidate is appointed.

Candidates often think their questions have not been answered even though the interviewer might think they have been. This seems to arise because the candidate feels that the interviewer was not really listening. This can be avoided if the interviewer practises 'active listening': listening with the ears, eyes and mind. Active listening includes taking account of NVC and doing an ongoing analysis of what you are being told. Active listening does not require you to simply act as a video recorder; it demands that you are immediately responsive to what you are recording. If you are following a set list of questions this can be difficult. It means breaking off and you can find that you lose the theme of the questions. Flexibility is, however, important. Candidates should not be alienated just so that you can keep to your schedule of questions. Active listening can be reflected in the response you give after an answer. Never say 'Okay', 'Right', or 'Well', and then go on to the next thing you want to ask. If nothing else, you should acknowledge the sentiment which has been expressed: 'you felt annoyed', 'you enjoyed it', 'you moved several times then', and so on. Also, avoid interrupting the candidate's answers mid-stream; which includes making sure that telephone calls or the arrival of your secretary do not interrupt them as well.

MAKING INTERNAL APPOINTMENTS

The discussion so far has been based on the assumption that the interview involves an external applicant. There are, however, many times when an internal candidate is considered for promotion against competition from outside. This introduces particular pressures for the interviewer.

Prospective internal applicants for a job must be given an especially clear explanation of the selection criteria so as to encourage realistic expectations of success. Where someone looks to be about to apply whom you know will not stand a chance, you might consider telling them informally about the strength of the opposition without stating that you knew they might apply. It is doubly important that anyone shortlisted actually has a chance of success. Sympathy shortlisting can backfire and can stimulate acrimony often directed at the successful applicant later.

Where two internal candidates apply for a job, it can be a problem. Do you tell them about each other? It is not in the interviewer's remit to make this decision. Only if they have agreed that their applications should be made public would the interviewer be justified in sharing this information.

An internal candidate unleashes different sorts of bias during interview. Knowledge, sometimes in-depth knowledge, of the candidate can engender liking or loathing. You have to examine how much of your feeling towards the candidate is relevant to his or her ability to do the job. Your past reactions to the person can make it very difficult to offer a fair hearing during the interview: you hear what experience has lead you to expect rather than what is said. A number of quite different motives come into play in handling internal applicants.

● The appointment might be an opportunity to get rid of someone you dislike or make room for someone you like better.

● You may feel that promotion for this person will act as a boost to morale for the others working with you.

- You may find the rise to success that this person is making is too fast, making you look slow.

- You might expect that the person would be grateful to you later and represent a useful contact elsewhere in the organisation.

- You might suspect that promotion of this person would create damaging envy in your other staff.

The list of motives is endless. Some produce bias in favour of internal applicants, others the reverse. There are few real remedies for such biases. The obvious one would be to exclude yourself from the selection process but this is rarely possible. It is more feasible to introduce co-interviewers to act as a counterweight to your biases. If you do so, you need to ensure they do not merely echo your own motivations.

During an interview with an internal candidate, it is vital that the same schedule of questions is asked. Shortcuts, because you think you know what they have done, or would say, should be avoided. Strict comparability with the information collected from other candidates should be sought.

BEING AN INTERNAL CANDIDATE

Internal applicants must themselves recognise that peculiar biases operate in such appointment decisions. It is important not to collude with them. It is necessary to approach the interview as you would any other with an outside organisation. Show your strengths as clearly as you can. Do not rely on your past performance to carry you through. It is also advisable to provide good references from outside the organisation.

In terms of internal appointments, women should take heart. There is a growing body of evidence which indicates that women stand a greater chance of gaining promotion within the organisation they work for than outside it. For men the relationship is reversed. It seems that some expectations about mobility operate here. Men prove themselves committed to their career by being willing to move; women do so by staying put.

INTERVIEWEE STRATEGIES

The interviewee should have a single objective in the interview, to get the job. Any doubt that you have about your own suitability for the job or, indeed, whether you want the job, should be left outside the interview room. If you carry doubt into the interview room, it will contaminate everything you say.

Once you fix on this single objective, it becomes relatively simple to decide on the line of self-presentation you should adopt. You will have established during the informal interview what profile the person appointed must match. You know the sorts of bias which operate during interviews to affect the evaluation of the candidate (see Box 3). Your task is to match the profile and turn the biases in your favour.

Matching the profile can be difficult. You may not have the qualifications or experience required. If this is so, but you still think you can do the job, you need to work out, prior to the interview, a series of statements which will show that you know how the job should be done and that the experience you do have is relevant. You might not be able to present your argument in one fell swoop but you should work to introduce your points, in turn, at appropriate times. Prior to the interview, you should also work out how you could substantiate these claims if they were challenged. Interviewers do not like to be regaled with a set piece of rhetoric; they like to think they are capable of making you think on your feet. Some of this apparent thinking on your feet can be done on your seat if you anticipate criticism. Practising the arguments with a friend who is briefed to act as an awkward interviewer can be both entertaining and profitable. It allows you to check phrasing, and is likely to help you to defuse anxiety.

Using the selection biases is in many ways less complex.

▶ If you know that selectors like all the space on the application form to be filled neatly, you fill it neatly.

▶ If you know that they tend to prefer dark masculine-type attire for a management interview, you wear it. You certainly don't turn up in a sweater and jeans. Flaunting convention can be fun, but it does not work nowadays.

▶ If they like attractive people, you can try to look your best: style your hair, wear your best jewellery, or have a particularly close shave. All these things can contribute to your own sense of confidence, irrespective of the impact they have on the interviewer.

▶ If you are aware that interviewers prefer people who are similar to themselves, use it. You can express agreement with views they espouse. If you do not know enough about them personally, make sure that you echo the values which characterise the organisation. You can use your own stereotypes of people with the interviewer's background to make some calculated guesses about what he or she might like and dislike.

▶ Remember too that it matters whether they are male or female. With a male interviewer, less self-disclosure is expected. With a female interviewer, you can afford to be a bit more non-traditional.

▶ If you know that interviewers are impressed by candidates who have prestigious connections, mention yours.

▶ If you know that they look for moderate levels of assertiveness in candidates, offer it to them. One way to do this is to use *powertalk*. It has been known for over ten years that usage of language differs between powerful and less powerful groups. Subordinate groups tend to use more:

- *questioning forms* (appending a verbal question mark to any statement): 'I think this, don't you?' 'Wouldn't you agree?' 'You know?'

- *hedges* (distancing themselves from their expressed opinions): 'at least it's possible that it sometimes might happen that way . . . '

- *hesitation* (umming, ahing, erring): 'I would . . . er . . . really . . . er . . . like this job, er.'

- *intensifiers* (exaggerating the statement made beyond the point where it sounds balanced): 'I know that I can do a really tremendous job for you, the challenge is so very marvellously exciting.'

These forms of speech tend to be cues for stereotyping. People using them are thought to be less honest, less persuasive, and certainly less assertive. An interviewee who wants to appear assertive without being aggressive needs to avoid such powerless forms of speech. Currently, women are more likely to use these forms than men.

If you can incorporate this knowledge about the selection biases operating at interview into your self-presentation, you should be one step further towards asserting some control. Control can also be achieved indirectly by helping the interviewer to become more relaxed. Showing that you have a sense of humour, making them smile, is important. This can be used to prevent the interview slipping into an interrogation. Push to make the interview interactive. Your objective is to make the interviewer see you as a potential colleague who would be worthy of respect, not just another candidate. In a long day of interviewing, the candidate with time for wry humour may have a better chance of being remembered. Of course, humour is a very personal thing and needs to be used carefully or it could backfire. The objective should not be to have them rolling in the aisles, just mildly conscious that, in a serious situation like the job interview, you have the time and reserves to see the need for some light relief.

Overcoming anxiety. Using strategies like these is only really possible if you can control your anxiety. Anxiety is normal in the interview situation. Up to a point it is advantageous – it sharpens your reflex wit – but beyond that point it can detract from performance. The symptoms of anxiety differ across people. They include: breathlessness, sweating, dry mouth, dizziness, irregular pulse beat, shakiness, wanting to vomit, urinate or defecate, difficulty with swallowing, sudden changes in body temperature and being unable to move. Some people experience chest pain or severe muscular tension, even blurring of vision. There are concomitant cognitive disorders too: memory decay, information processing restrictions, and the intrusion of thoughts irrelevant to the immediate situation.

Experiencing such symptoms can be very frightening. The first thing is to recognise that they are intensified if you panic and start to think you are physically ill. Label the symptoms properly: they stem from anxiety and will subside if you can relax. Relaxation can be achieved by an effort of will. Control your breathing first. Regularise it: take deep paced breaths. Anxiety often results in quick, shallow breaths, with negative physiological effects. If you cannot consciously control the breathing, get a paper bag or something similar and cover your mouth with it. Breathing in the bag for a short time will reduce your oxygen intake and calm you physiologically. It is easy enough to keep a paper bag in your pocket just in case. Muscular relaxation should be attempted too. Relax each muscle of your body in turn starting with the toes. This becomes easier with practice – regular, even daily, practice can help generally with stress management (see Fontana, 1989, for detailed information on managing stress).

There is another approach which you can take in handling anxiety. This focuses upon the causes not the symptoms. This entails considering how you normally feel before and during an interview and trying to pinpoint the thoughts which accompany your anxiety. Very often these thoughts reflect self-doubt. You feel you are no good. You think you cannot cope. You think you will make a fool of yourself. If these are the thoughts which plague you before an interview, one way to tackle them is to analyse your performance rationally. Admittedly, the analysis should be somewhat biased to accentuate your achievements and good points. So you might ask yourself:

? What good things have I achieved so far in my career?

? Why are they interviewing me if I'm no good?

? What interviews have I done well in before?

? In what ways do I match their ideal candidate?

? In what ways am I better than the other candidates?

Focus your efforts on retrieving and thinking about your successes. The emphasis on the positive self-image can block the self-doubt and make you feel that little bit more confident on entering the interview. It can reduce your overall level of anxiety so that the increase in anxiety you experience when you go into the interview is not disabling (for further details of this method for controlling anxiety, see Edelmann, 1987).

GIVING FEEDBACK AFTER THE INTERVIEW

It is still quite rare for external candidates to be given feedback, though it is happening now more often in teaching. It is good practice to provide it, if requested. It may also be useful to offer it unsolicited: educating the pool of potential candidates is in everyone's long-term interests. Feedback should be factual and specific, not simplistic exhortations for change. It should indicate what additional qualifications or experience the candidate needs before re-applying for this sort of job. It should indicate the questions which seemed to cause the candidate most trouble and what type of answers were expected.

In order to begin to understand what type of feedback is useful, you might try to list the things which you would have liked to be told about after your own last interview. Some of these would probably never be provided by the interviewer; some would be permissible. Next time you interview someone, try to give them equivalent sorts of information.

INTERPRETING INFORMATION

How information gathered during selection interviewing can be interpreted has not been examined above. Obviously, the ultimate decision must be based on an assessment of how far each candidate satisfies the selection criteria. The use of weighted ratings against the selection criteria, suggested earlier, systematises this task. However, there are other factors to consider when interpreting information from interviews. These are described at the end of Chapter 4.

Chapter Four

Selection Panels and Group Interviews

In many situations, selection interviewing involves more than one interviewer. Instead, two or more interviewers comprise a panel. This
chapter examines how these panels operate and how their operation
can be optimised. It is also the case that group interviewing is increasingly used in selection procedures and a brief introduction is provided
to what they entail and their value.

WHY USE PANELS TO INTERVIEW?

In many cases, an organisation insists that interviews entail an appointments board that forms, in effect, an interview panel. Most senior posts
involve panel interviews and there are other occasions when it is useful
to have a panel rather than a one-to-one interview even when it is not
required by the organisation. These include:

● Where the individual advertising a post feels that the interests of
several groups or sections within the organisation need to be protected
when the appointment is made. Representatives of a number of dispa-
rate viewpoints can then be included in the panel.

● Where other members of the organisation have particular expertise
needed in assessing candidates. If this is the case, whoever is chosen
might be consulted at the job analysis stage and in the establishment
of the selection criteria.

● Where the individual advertising the post is eager to prevent any
bias in the selection.

● Where the fact of the appointment needs to be publicised or accepted within the broader organisation. The panel can be used to emphasise the fairness of the selection procedure.

ORGANISING THE PANEL

If they are to be effective, panels need to be well organised.

MEMBERSHIP

Each member of a panel should have a role to perform; superfluous members can be a nuisance. The typical panel membership for any reasonably senior post would probably include: the appointee's immediate line manager or supervisor to provide information about the job and an evaluation of candidates in terms of that specific job; a member of the personnel department to provide information on local conditions of employment and any legal details; someone from elsewhere in the organisation (possibly from a different professional group) to ask broad-ranging questions of general interest; and someone with expertise relevant to the candidates' field of interest (possibly from outside the organisation). In addition, there would typically be a chairperson, usually drawn from the senior management of the organisation.

SIZE OF PANELS

Panels numbering more than five become unwieldy. The interviews become long because everyone has to ask a question and the time for answering is correspondingly shortened. Factions can develop. Supporters of one candidate vie with those of another. Individuals are more likely to use the interview as a venue to settle old scores. It is more difficult to timetable the interview because so many diaries have to be consulted. Larger panels are also much more threatening to candidates. The fundamental rule should be: never have more people on the panel than you absolutely need. A subsidiary rule would be: always have an odd number; if it comes to a vote, no draw should be possible. Of course, the chair can always reserve the casting vote.

JOBS FOR THE PANEL

The role of the panel in the selection process can be as extensive or as limited as you like. Every member can be consulted on the job description and selection criteria or just some of them; they can be asked to help in shortlisting; they can be introduced only in the final phase of interviewing. Again in the absence of any organisational norms, parsimony should be the rule. Only use a panel where members offer something more than you would otherwise have available in terms of information, influence, or experience.

SCHEDULING THE QUESTIONS

There is considerable disagreement about the degree of freedom individual panel members should have in deciding their questions. In some types of panel the schedule of questions is fairly fixed, prior to the start, either by whoever establishes the selection criteria or in prior discussion by the entire panel. This has advantages over offering members total freedom. It ensures that everything that needs to be covered actually gets asked and means that weighting of selection criteria is possible. It precludes confusing overlap in questions and it should produce a set of questions which have some rational connection or flow. Members have a clear understanding of their areas of responsibility in the interview and can avoid trespassing into another's territory unwittingly.

The disadvantages are two-fold. It can interfere with flexibility too much – the candidate recognises that the interviewers are not following a spontaneous line of argument. And it can be difficult to achieve. Even if they agree initially to the schedule, they often forget in the heat of the interview. A workable compromise would involve setting the areas to be covered by each panel member but then leaving them to think up their own questions. This can introduce great variability across candidates as the panel tires of asking the same questions for the fifth time and starts to try a little lateral thinking. A chairperson must monitor the boredom factor and intervene. Panels are more likely to keep to the set list of topics if they understand and accept that they reflect the selection criteria.

REACHING A DECISION

This really brings us to the final task: reaching a decision. If the selection criteria are explicit and weighted for their importance, it should be possible for panel members to rate the candidate against them in the manner described in Chapter 3. There can be minor variations: for instance, each member might be asked to rate only in some areas, normally those on which they are particularly knowledgeable. The real problem then comes in pooling these individual judgements to generate a decision. There are several commonly-used ways.

❏ The simplest way is to let each member decide (according to their own ratings) which candidate should be appointed. They then have a single vote and the candidate with the most votes gets the job offer. The rating leading to their individual choice can be made either with or without a discussion between panel members. Making ratings without prior discussion reduces the risk of the most powerful member of the panel having excessive influence. It is a hedge against conformity pressures which operate in any group decision-making. Of course, cutting the discussion will reduce the opportunities for airing alternative viewpoints which may also be important. One way to handle this dilemma is to have members state publicly their initial vote and then open the discussion. After that, if relevant arguments are made, votes may be recast.

❏ The model above may be used with a modificiation which gives one panel member (normally the immediate line manager/supervisor) more weight in the vote (maybe the equivalent of a veto).

❏ Some members of the panel may be present in a non-voting, consultative role. Their opinions are voiced but they have no final vote. This has to be made clear to them at the outset.

Whichever decision-making method is adopted, members should always be expected to substantiate their opinion with detailed reasons. Opinions based largely on stereotypes or other biases are then less likely to be paraded.

The decision-making model actually chosen will depend on the nature of the job to be filled and the organisation's standard procedures. In many cases, panels will be making not one but several appointments from a pool of candidates interviewed at the same time. In this situation, it may be necessary to supplement the rating system with one that rank orders candidates.

It is important where several jobs are available to establish the minimum requirements in an appointee so that all interviewers can recognise those applicants who cannot be accepted even if they are reasonably high in the rank ordering. It is worth consciously deciding what system you want to use in each panel interview you organise.

CHAIRING A PANEL INTERVIEW

The chair must take responsibility for setting the candidate at ease and clarifying any misunderstandings which arise either because the panel is contradictory in the information members give the candidate or because the candidate fails to assimilate information. Equally, if a panel member has clearly misunderstood an answer the chair should intervene quickly to clarify.

Individual members of a panel will find it difficult to exert control over a candidate so that, if one shows signs of blathering, the chair needs to step in. A few words will often re-orientate them: for example, 'I think perhaps you misunderstand the thrust of . . . 's question'; 'You have not really answered the central question which was . . . '.

Normally, a chair will brief the panel before the first candidate arrives on the ground rules which are to operate. In particular, the chair must ensure that members know their roles and know how a decision will be made. They need to be told before they start what will happen in the event of a disagreement on the choice of candidate. If the single vote per member system is operating, the chair should be able to resolve any deadlock with a casting vote.

Chairing panel interviews for internal candidates, particularly in the context of promotions, may be tricky. Such events normally trigger hidden animosities and it is important for the chair to clear the decks of any internal disputes at the start. It is always useful to have spoken to the immediate line manager/supervisor before the interview. In such cases, it may be necessary to state what types of information about the candidate will be regarded as permissible.

Given the power attached to any chairperson, it is likely that the chair's opinions will carry considerable weight in the panel. A chair can minimise conformity by refraining from expressing an opinion until all other members have done so. For the same reason, it may be wise to ask for the opinion of the most junior member of the panel first.

PANEL INTERVIEWS: THE CANDIDATE'S PERSPECTIVE

For the interviewees, panel interviews have all of the problems of the one-to-one interview and some more. The problem of analysing the ideal profile for the job is there and so are the various selection biases. The same self-presentation tactics which were described earlier can be used. The main additional problem is that you may be faced with several different, perhaps conflicting, expectations within the panel. Role portrayal becomes a nightmare because to please one, you offend another. There are some tactics which can help.

1. Be consistent in your answers: do not try to conform to what you think the question demands. Your answers should be consistent with each other and with the image of yourself you wish to portray.

2. If you see that two members of the panel are clearly in conflict in their approach or beliefs, try not to take sides. Show that you recognise the conflict. Illustrate that you understand the pros and cons of the arguments being made and come to a balanced stance which is consistent with the self-image you are portraying.

3. Answer each person's question directly. Do not get trapped by the desire to hark back to earlier questions except to show consistency in your approach.

4. If a question is difficult, say that you think it is difficult and why. Use this time to work out your response. Interviewers like to be told they have asked a good question. You can also ingratiate yourself with interviewers by expressing agreement with them in a differentiated way. This basically entails being willing to express mild disagreement on very minor issues but unswerving agreement on big issues.

5. Never be afraid to use humour. Showing that you can see the lighter side of an issue and then offering the serious meat of your argument has impact; and this is important. You want to stand out from the mass.

6. Do not allow an aggressive panel to harass you. Panels can do this in a number of ways: by asking questions in quick succession (often ones which contradict each other); by interrupting your answers with challenges; by carrying on side conversations; by looking meaningfully at each other as you answer; and so on. Recognise that this may be a deliberate ploy to see how you handle stress. If this is likely, you could say that you think that this might be happening and then continue your answer. For the situation where many questions come in quickfire succession, take a pen and paper into the interview and jot down the main points you need to make in your response. If you have to disagree with a panel member, do so politely. It is fatal to show impatience or lose your temper in an interview. Don't get angry, get analytical.

GROUP INTERVIEWS

There is a trend towards selection procedures which allow candidates to be observed doing different tasks with other people; goal-directed communication can then be monitored. They are a condensed variant of the assessment centre used in industry, the armed forces and the civil service to choose personnel, particularly high flyers and senior management. These truncated assessments usually take one full day.

Candidates for a job (normally four or five) are brought together at the start of the day, briefed on the job and the organisation and presented with a number of tasks to do during the day. Some of the tasks will require them to work alone. For others they have to work together with one or more other candidates. Once the tasks are completed they normally then face a panel interview. The tasks are designed to assess the skills or knowledge demanded by the selection criteria. For any management or senior administrative post these normally include:

The ability to interpret and use information. The task here might involve being presented with data about the sort of department they would manage if appointed and being asked how they would proceed to solve a number of problems in the department, giving the rationale for their solution.

The ability to liaise with others in solving problems. This task might involve giving each candidate part of the information necessary for the solution of a complex problem and asking them to reach the optimal solution in a fixed time.

The ability to communicate effectively. The task here could be to present the solutions from Task 1 to the selectors and the other candidates in a persuasive and lucid way; it might include having to comment publicly on each others' solutions.

The ability to think creatively. This is often tested using a practical problem: 'How would you get from point A to point B, 500 miles apart, with only one pound, a Mars bar, and a pen knife?'

The precise nature of the tasks is irrelevant. It is rarely the solutions to the puzzles or the decisions reached in debate that interest the selectors. The object is to observe how candidates get to that point. The aim is to see how they reason, how they communicate; not what they think; not what they say.

In the right hands, this assessment centre approach is a very powerful tool. It can give a rich insight into the way people operate. It is infinitely superior to the interview alone because it allows direct observation of behaviour and you are not dependent merely upon the self-description of the candidate.

However, analysis of this sort of behavioural data is notoriously problematic. It is subject to every imaginable bias in the observer. A selector needs extensive training to use the approach properly. It is inadvisable to use it unless you have that training.

CANDIDATES facing assessment exercises need to remember a number of things.

1. Analyse which ability each task is designed to test. Do not become preoccupied with the minutiae of the task itself, but rather focus upon exemplifying the ability it is designed to tap. For example, if the task involves the ability to communicate to a group concentrate upon your presentation, use any audio-visual aids available, marshal all your non-verbal skills to carry your argument to the audience, use powertalk, and so on.

2. Note the weaknesses of your competitors, especially where they do not match the ideal selection profile and help them to display their weaknesses in the group tasks. For example, you might suggest that a person, who clearly has no head for figures, does the statistical analysis of the hypothetical budget you have been given. They will probably back out; do not push them. This way you score doubly: first, by pointing to their weakness and, second, by noting the weakness and showing leadership ability in persuading someone more able to do the job.

3. Do not let real emotions become aroused. You may need to pretend distress or pleasure but keep it on the surface. The interactions in the tasks are all contrived to observe you. Your objective is to portray what the observers wish to see. Real emotions cloud your ability to do this. In particular, you should avoid expressing boredom. This is typically interpreted as a lack of commitment to the job.

4. Do not believe the selectors will do what they have said they will do. Expect sudden changes to the day's timetable; this may be designed to test flexibility.

5. Accept that the other candidates may also wish to mislead you – maintain a healthy, friendly suspicion. You may be asked to socialise with the other candidates over lunch or dinner and you may be observed at that time too. You will be expected to present the out-of-work characteristics associated with the job during that time. For instance, the ability to talk sensibly about world issues, non-comittally about politics, and interestingly on sport or theatre. It is important not to slip into isolation during these social aspects of the assessment. It is easy to do so if you are nervous. The anxiety management techniques described earlier can help if you focus on the positive aspects of your ability in such situations.

6. When an interview follows a package of assessment tasks, it will often include reference to your earlier performance. Again, try to maintain consistency of self-presentation. You may be asked to offer assessments of other candidates with reference to the tasks; give a balanced

(pros and cons) answer. Make sure that anything which you wished to convey about your suitability for the job, and which has been missed in the exercises, is said at interview. Try to anticipate any queries about disparities in your performance during the exercises and your record on paper. Work out in advance what you need to say to resolve any inconsistencies.

7. These assessment exercises are tiring, mentally and physically. Pace yourself; use relaxation exercises unobtrusively during breaks; do not forget to eat something at lunch, and so on. Your objective is to have something left in reserve for the interview at the end of the day.

Remembering these tactics should help you handle such group assessments. They demand, however, great skill in self-presentation which really only comes with practice. You might want to do a trial run for a job which you would not mind losing to get experience.

VALIDITY AND RELIABILITY OF SELECTION INTERVIEW ASSESSMENTS

Validity refers to the extent to which an assessment technique measures what it is supposed to measure. There are two main types of validity. The first is construct validity which focuses upon achieving a measure which is valid even if it looks unlikely. For instance, individual differences in the length of an optical illusion called the spiral after-effect is a good index of extroversion – unlikely though it may seem. The second is face validity which concentrates upon achieving an index which at face value looks as though it has something to do with the thing to be measured. So, for instance, one might ask someone whether they like parties and use this as an index of extroversion.

The types of question asked in interviews often have face validity – they appear, on the surface, to be tapping what they seek to measure. However, they frequently have little construct validity. They are not really accessing the correct information. This may be because a candidate lies or gives partly truthful answers. It may be because a question which is ostensibly about one thing actually raises other issues as well. For instance, a question about willingness to take on responsibility may be answered negatively but it would be rash to assume therefore that the candidate did not want more responsibility at work. It may be that this answer was a product of the candidate's current domestic responsibilities. Questions designed to tap personality are particularly subject to problems of construct validity. We know from extensive studies that interviewers are very poor judges of personality and are not very good at predicting work-related abilities from their interview questions. Judgements based on application forms alone produce equally good or bad results.

Interview assessments also have problems with reliability. Reliability, in this context, refers to the extent to which a question produces the same measurement of a characteristic over time with the same person or across interviewers who ask it. It can also refer to the extent to which a question will elicit comparable information across candidates. Most of the questions used in selection interviewing have never been seriously tested for reliability. Where attempts have been made, again it has been shown that questions directed at the important areas of personality, communication skills, and leadership ability have limited reliability. For instance, questioning is often directed at ascertaining how well someone handles pressure (in the guise of heavy workloads or unpredictable events). Direct questions such as 'How would you handle an emergency such as a student disappearing during a school visit?'; or, 'How do you react to having to do very long shifts?'; or, 'Do you have difficulty with your current caseload?'; tend to evoke different types of answer depending on who asks them and when in the interview the candidate answers them. It depends on how the interviewer reacted to the last answer, the tone of voice used in asking the question, the pattern of previous answers, the point in the interview at which it is asked, the expectations aroused in the candidate about the type of question to expect, and so on.

The biggest problem is unreliability across different interviewers. This is a major issue where several interviewers are each asked to interview a different batch of candidates (something which happens frequently for low-level appointments). Even when interviewers can be trained to ask the same questions in the same order, it is difficult to train them to interpret answers given in comparable ways. The same answer to the same question will mean different things to different interviewers. Some of this can be eradicated by training based on offering them standard ways to interpret standard answers. The best way to do this is interactively. For instance, a group of potential interviewers is shown a series of videotaped interviews using the specific schedule of questions they need to learn. They are told what each question is designed to tap and how answers should be interpreted. They watch the videotaped interviews and rate the candidates on the selection criteria. They do this individually and then discuss their interpretations. Idiosyncratic interpretations or ratings are highlighted and the interviewer producing them is expected to change. Repeated practice sessions will introduce some reliability across interviewers. It is a way to give each candidate a fair chance. Since interviewers will slip back into individual prejudices if not monitored, updating training sessions are valuable.

In selection interviewing these worrying facts need to be borne in mind. They should not, however, be over-emphasised. Interviews may be an imperfect form of assessment but, on the whole, they are no worse than other methods. It is also worth bearing in mind that selection interviews may serve many useful functions in an organisation besides their manifest purpose, allowing the recruitment process to become highly visible to staff at various levels, and providing them frequently with the opportunity to comment upon it. As long as selection interviews have ulterior benefits, it will be worthwhile for everyone concerned to try to make them more effective.

Chapter Five

Appraisal Interviews

With the shift to management by objectives in the caring professions and in education, most practitioners can expect to become involved in appraisal interviewing at some time; both appraising others and being appraised.

THE PURPOSE OF APPRAISAL INTERVIEWS

The overall purpose of an appraisal interview is to evaluate current staff performance and determine what they should be doing next. The appraisal interview breaks down into three parts:

1. Setting objectives and negotiating performance indicators. Appraisal interviews are used to discuss the objectives which the person needs to achieve within a set time period. Organisations differ in the extent to which they impose objectives or make them subject to negotiation with the staff members concerned. In most contexts now where professionals operate, appraisal is a cooperative enterprise and the objectives are set jointly after consultation. Nevertheless, even in the education, health and social services, there will be organisational expectations which have to be fulfilled. As various forms of management by objectives become the norm, it is predictable that flexibility in the setting of objectives will be diminished, and objectives will be set more centrally according to a management plan.

Once objectives are determined, they have to be tied to performance indicators. Each of these should be an agreed index of how far an objective has been achieved. There can be any number of performance indicators. For example, if one of the objectives agreed with the head of the English department in a school is to increase the extra-curricular activities of that department, one of the performance indicators might be organising a school play. Similarly, if a social services locality team manager has, as an objective, the improvement of services for the elderly in the area, the performance indicators might include appointing new staff with responsibility for the elderly, arranging training for existing staff on the needs of the elderly, and so on. If the objectives set for a staff nurse include becoming skilled in intensive care techniques, successful completion of an appropriate training course could be used as a performance indicator.

2. *Review of performance against previously-established indicators.* Performance indicators need to be specific and unambiguous. When you come to review performance against the indicators it needs to be clear whether or not they have been achieved.

The appraisal interview must examine both successes and failures on performance indicators. Rewards for success (even if only praise) and punishments for failure (even if only criticism) should be built into the appraisal process.

3. *Deciding what changes in performance are needed and the plan of action required to achieve them.* Analysing what changes are desirable and feasible and how they can be achieved is the central task for the appraisal interview. It links in with setting objectives and picking performance indicators. The analysis itself, however, requires somewhat different skills. Pin-pointing where change is needed and translating that into definable objectives are different parts of the process.

At the outset of an appraisal interview, both parties need to be clear what outcomes are possible. These might include firing, promotion, more pay, provision of training, or simply personal satisfaction for a job acknowledged to be well done. Appraisal interviews are tied into different reward systems across organisations. It is worth noting that appraisal which carries no reward/punishment implications can be de-motivating. The appraisal becomes merely an exchange of views between two people who may be meeting on a regular basis anyway to organise how the job should be done.

HOW TO PREPARE YOURSELF FOR APPRAISAL

You can get the most out of appraisal by doing some preparation. Appraisals normally cover a specified period of time (for example, the last year or six months) and, in preparing for an appraisal interview, you need to assess your own performance over that time. An appraisal should be used as an occasion to spend some time thinking about your own achievements and goals. Set aside time, prior to the interview, to think through what you are doing and want to do next.

This process is often facilitated by having to complete an appraisal questionnaire in advance. This is designed to provide initial detailed information for the appraiser and it is likely to include both what you have been doing and what you would like to do next.

Use self-evaluation. If you have had appraisal interviews before, you will know what objectives have been set and the relevant performance indicators. Self-evaluation is therefore more directed though it is always worth considering whether the objectives were realistic and the performance indicators were appropriate. The appraiser may be unaware of salient facts that have vitiated the original plan. You should make yourself ready to articulate changes in circumstances which affected your achievement of objectives. It is, however, unwise to rely upon 'unanticipated circumstances' to explain failures. One of the features of the management by objectives approach is that staff are expected to report quickly when they are being thwarted in achieving objectives by unforeseen events. The organisation can then act to remove the obstacle or objectives can be altered.

If you have never had an appraisal interview in this job before, you can try to list the goals which you have pursued during the specified period. You should analyse your own strengths and weaknesses. Where have you succeeded? Where have you failed? Why did you succeed? Why did you fail?

This analysis will allow you to go into the appraisal interview with ideas about where you might like to focus your future activities. This might mean concentrating on those things you do well. It might mean trying to eliminate areas of weakness by further training. It might reveal that you really want a complete change; you have been doing the same task for too long and it no longer stimulates you.

It is important in doing this self-evaluation to allow yourself to take your feelings into account. The management by objectives approach can ignore the whole realm of feelings. You may be very good and productive at a job, achieving the objectives set, satisfying performance indicators, but still be unhappy. If you are unhappy, you need to ask yourself why. If you can determine the reason, you can assess how best to deal with it, and this strategy would be included in your plan of action for the next period of time. If the source is beyond your immediate control (for example, a manager you find unreasonable) you might wish to discuss this in the appraisal interview.

Know what you want to say. Go into the appraisal interview with a clear idea of what you want to say. You might work out a shopping list of things which you want to cover. Have concrete suggestions to make about how you can introduce the changes which you would like to see. For instance, do not ask for some such general goal as 'more responsibility and autonomy' without knowing what that means in practice. Which new things could you take over? What would be the drawbacks in the change? How can they be overcome? If you need evidence to support your assertions, have it ready and, if possible, take it with you. Always have contingency suggestions ready to fall back on if your prime target for change is rejected.

You can resist an objective or a performance indicator which you do not like. The level of resistance that is feasible will doubtless reflect the rewards and punishments available to the appraiser. Strong and persistent resistance during an appraisal which results in momentary embarrassment may save you months of regret later. Take time to consider objectives which are suggested to you and look at their problems as well as their simpler aspects. Make the problems known to the appraiser. You are the expert in the job you do; the appraiser may not have anticipated all the problems in the suggested objective.

Don't make snap decisions in the appraisal. If you cannot decide during the appraisal whether an objective is achievable, agree to do a feasibility analysis. You could check on whether other people in similar organisations have been able to achieve such objectives. It might involve breaking the objective into sub-goals and seeing how long it takes to complete the first part. For instance, if the objective for a head teacher was to change the image of the school in the local community, this could be broken into a number of sub-goals: improving parent involvement in the school; getting pupils to achieve better grades in exams; encouraging more community use of school buildings out of school hours; etc. This sort of breakdown into sub-goals is useful in giving you some idea of the timescale involved in achieving an objective. The appraisal should give you an opportunity to negotiate a realistic timescale for objectives.

— APPRAISING YOURSELF —

EXERCISE 4

Work through each question in turn. Make your answers explicit; produce them in such a way that someone else would understand what you think. Where relevant, use the last 12 months as the period of assessment.

1. **What do you consider to be the major areas of your activity at work?** (These might include direct contact with patients, clients or students; acquiring new skills; management of staff; educating junior staff; administration; forward planning of service provision, and so on.)

2. **How have you distributed your time across these areas?** (Try to work out the percentages.)

3. **In each area, what were your objectives?** How far have you achieved them and how do you feel about your own performance? (Specify – pride, anger, worry, etc., and its intensity.) What were your major successes in the year?

4. **What factors have limited you?** (These can include personal circumstances or attributes as well as organisational constraints.)

5. **What positive measures can be taken,** either by you or the organisation, to improve your performance?

6. **What new areas would you like to move into?** (Be precise about this. What are the obstacles which hinder you? How realistic is it to expect to be able to move into these areas?)

7. **What areas would you like to drop?** (How can this be arranged?)

8. **Are you on course in terms of your career timetable?** (How does what you are doing now and what you would like to do next fit with your overall career plans? If not, where do you think you have to put your greatest effort?)

It is important in completing the self-appraisal to lend as much weight to your successes as your failures. People have a tendency to underplay success and overemphasise failure. Be wary of falling into this trap.

ACTING AS AN APPRAISER

The initial problem for an appraiser is to know what objectives to set and which performance indicators to use. If the organisation has clear guidelines there is less of a problem. In the main, however, organisations rely upon individual appraisers to elaborate specific objectives and indicators against a backdrop of general guidelines. The easiest way to proceed is to use a job analysis and to refer to the past experience of the incumbent. You know then what has to be achieved in the job and something of the practical constraints which apply.

You may also wish to take into account the talent and character of the current incumbent in shaping the objectives once they have been set. Unless you want a reason to fire someone, it is pointless setting objectives which the individual would find totally unachievable. Objectives should be set at such a level that the person is stretched but not snapped.

You have to go into the appraisal knowing what objectives you want to establish. You have to have them clearly formulated and be able to describe them explicitly, translating them into concrete performance indicators. This does not preclude negotiation with the person you are appraising about the objectives and indicators but it does mean that you start from a definite base.

Appraisals must include firm statements of what you find good and bad in a person's previous performance, giving your reasons. You will normally use the appraisal questionnaire, completed before the interview, to give you detailed information. In the main, your evaluation will be done against performance indicators agreed at the start of the period you are reviewing. However, there will always be incidental comments about performance which are needed in areas not covered by the specified performance indicators. For instance, in the case of a mental health specialist working for the social services, involvement in the local marriage guidance council's work need not have been included in the performance indicators set, but it would be useful to acknowledge its value in the appraisal.

Having reviewed achievements, you have to outline what needs to be done next. If a person has done well, you can choose to consolidate their performance at that level or to push him or her further. Either way, it is useful to arrange some reward to maintain motivation: for example, some increment in resources or recognition of promotion prospects. Maintaining motivation in the absence of material reward is not easy. Some of the education and caring professions have relied upon the professional or vocational ethic to do this in the past. In many ways,

APPRAISAL FEEDBACK

EXERCISE 5

It is relatively easy to give feedback to a member of staff who is achieving set objectives. This exercise allows you to practise giving feedback to someone who is failing. Choose someone that works with you, who would fall into this category, and work through the feedback proforma below filling in what you would say to that person. You should concentrate upon the precise way you would tell them. You have to maintain an atmosphere of constructive, unbiased comment. The methods of delivering the information will depend on the temperament of the person you are dealing with but waffle, hesitation and self-contradiction must be avoided at all costs.

FEEDBACK PROFORMA

1 What were the objectives set and the performance indicators used?

2 Which objectives were met and missed? What have been the implications of these successes and failures? (Rate the relative importance of each. Arrive at an overall evaluation for the year's performance.)

3 How would you genuinely offer praise for the successes?

4 Summarise the reasons for failure which have become evident in the appraisal. How would you state these without becoming threatening? Make it clear, where necessary, that you know they may have occurred because the person is dependent upon others doing their job properly (including perhaps yourself).

5 Summarise the changes needed (personal and organisational). Again, how would you do this without becoming aggressive? If there are a number of changes to be made, know how you would prioritise them.

6 Specify the rewards and punishments contingent upon subsequent performance. Make clear what organisational resources are available to support the changes.

the management by objectives approach is antithetical to recourse to value systems to justify actions. It may erode motivation levels over the long term unless accompanied by a system of material, or at least socially-valued, rewards.

If staff have had difficulty in achieving objectives, you need to establish what can be done to help them improve and what remedial steps can be taken. If performance is very weak you need to try to understand why. It may not be advisable for a particular individual to continue in this job. This should be considered as an option where remedial measures fail, but should only be applied after a series of warnings.

Where new objectives are being considered, the appraiser should attempt to show clearly and explicitly how they are in the interests of both the organisation and the appraisee. Imposition of objectives can result in deliberate or unconscious sabotage by the staff. Explanation of the objectives is one way to encourage their acceptance. If it fails, other inducements can be used. If this fails, the appraiser again has to consider the use of sanctions. If sanctions are likely to be needed, you need to decide what they will be and how they will be applied before you enter the appraisal. The range of formal sanctions available is normally laid down by the organisation.

The appraisal should allow time and room for the manager to be given feedback. This can include comments on organisational constraints, colleague problems, and management inefficiency. The comments have the greatest impact if they are phrased constructively and the general ethos of the appraisal should encourage honesty in the knowledge that no recriminations will be allowed. People find it hard to accept that they can criticise without recriminations. This suspicion can only be broken down gradually over a series of appraisals. It will be banished sooner if the appraiser always fulfils promises made in the interview. For example, if someone needs certain experience or training to achieve certain goals and this is offered during the appraisal, it should then be provided without fail. Promises should not be given lightly. If your ability to keep a promise is dependent upon other people, tell the appraisee at the time.

Appraisals will engender greater honesty if it is understood that they are completely confidential. Subsequent maintenance of confidentiality, perhaps over several years, must also be assured. Legislation which gives employees access to their own computerised records might also affect what the appraiser wishes to record in that way.

It is useful, when concluding an appraisal interview, to summarise what has been agreed. This summary is typically written down and both people sign it as an accurate record of the appraisal. Neither is then reliant on the fallibility of memory if disputes arise.

CHOOSING AN APPRAISER

Appraisers are normally the immediate line manager or supervisor but this can be varied. Some organisations allow appraisees to choose their own appraiser. If this happens, choosing someone other than your manager or supervisor has pros but also cons.

Pros: You may feel that previous disagreements with your immediate boss will result in biases in the appraisal. You may feel your boss does not possess the expertise necessary to give you advice on your next career step. You may feel that repeated interviews over several years with the same boss have brought you to the point where you want a change, particularly if you feel little progress has been made over the last few appraisals.

Cons: Someone else may know too little about your work to give accurate guidance in setting objectives. Someone else may be unable to transmit your criticisms or comments to your boss and thus have an impact on your work. Turning to someone else might feel like an act of betrayal to your boss.

If given the choice, it may be worth considering a compromise where you use your immediate manager or supervisor in the first instance but arrange for a referee if there is real disagreement. The referee would not be present at the first appraisal interview but would provide a second appraisal if you were dissatisfied. Recourse to a referee is clearly a major step, not to be taken lightly because it may alienate you from your manager (and even your colleagues), but it is an option you would normally have available. In case a referee is needed, it is useful to have decided at the outset who it will be. Obviously it has to be someone respected by both sides.

SKILLS REQUIRED IN APPRAISAL INTERVIEWING

Appraisal interviewing is very different from selection interviewing because it is done within the context of an ongoing working relationship. It will occur iteratively probably between the same people over several years. Both parties in the appraisal interview rely upon skills of negotiation, hopefully used in a cooperative enterprise. This requires the development of mutual trust and honesty. Decisions made in the appraisal can affect the working relationship for longer periods of time. It is therefore essential to take the task seriously, establishing achievable, agreed objectives which can be measured against known performance indicators, with adequate feedback on sucesses and failures, and sensible interventions to provide support.

Chapter Six

Research Interviews

Interviewing is an essential part of most types of social research. It is particularly prevalent in 'action research' or 'programme evaluation' research. Members of the health, education and social services are becoming interested in this sort of research. They want to evaluate the effectiveness of their own work and to explore systematically how it might be improved. A nurse might want to know whether patients are understanding instructions they are given about medication. A teacher might want to know whether some sorts of project work are better than others in encouraging skill acquisition. A local police force might want to know if 'neighbourhood watch' is improving community relations in an area. A social worker might want to know if the people in a home for the elderly are satisfied with the meals since they have been provided by a subcontractor. In each case, the practitioners want to know something about the impact of the work they do. The best way to find out is to interview the people they serve.

This chapter describes how research interviewing is done and how information derived from it can be handled. It will be evident, by the end, that the skills needed in research interviewing overlap with those used in selection or appraisal interviewing. Gaining expertise in one area will improve performance in the others.

ACTION RESEARCH AND PROGRAMME EVALUATION

Action research is a label which covers all sorts of activity. Ideally, it is a piece of research designed to initiate some change in the people, the organisations, or the procedures, studied. In other words it has an objective, normally to produce development or improvement. It is not simply aimed at producing a description of what already exists; it is aimed at changing it. For instance, research done by the police force to assess the impact of a neighbourhood watch scheme would become 'action' research if, as a consequence of it, the scheme was modified (for example, more people became involved, those involved were more satisfied with their contacts with the police).

Programme evaluation is one variant of action research. Typically, it involves monitoring how an organisation operates or how services are provided, estimating how they might be improved, introducing changes and calculating the effects these have.

This chapter focuses upon how interviewing can be used in action research or programme evaluation in the context of the education, health and social service professions. The argument was made in Chapter 1 that with the introduction of new management structures and financial restraints, individual practitioners may need to use the results of research to support claims for resources and to prove efficiency to themselves, the public and their employers.

DESIGNING RESEARCH

The design of any research project entails 4 stages:

▶ 1. Specifying what you want to know.

▶ 2. Deciding who you need information from.

▶ 3. Choosing the way you will collect the information.

▶ 4. Establishing how you will analyse the results.

WHAT DO YOU WANT TO KNOW?

You need to formulate very clear questions that you would like to answer with your research. You might start with a broad area of concern but it then has to be broken down into its component parts which can be stated very clearly. For instance, you may feel that you have failed to respond adequately to the problem that AIDS/HIV represents to your activities and that you could do more to provide information for your students, patients or clients. The research questions here might include:

? What does the group (whether clients, patients or students) with whom you work know about AIDS/HIV and the risks of infection?

? What information do you currently provide?

? What effects do your current efforts have in improving knowledge or changing behaviour?

? How could you improve the quality or quantity of information most effectively?

? Does the group want you to provide more information?

Once your questions get to this level of specificity it is possible to move on to the next stage of design.

WHO DO YOU NEED TO ASK?

The specific research questions determine which people you will ask for information. There are different types of sampling strategy you can use.

'Population sampling': this entails taking all of the people who share the characteristics which interest you (this could be all of the group you work with). Unless the numbers in this population are very small, this will be impossible for you.

'Random sampling': this is a way of scaling down the numbers you have to deal with and entails drawing individuals at random out of the overall population that interests you: every person has an equal chance of being studied. You might take every tenth, or every one hundredth, from an alphabetical list.

'Representative sampling': this entails ensuring that subsections of your overall population are represented in your final sample in the same proportions in which they appear in your overall population. For instance, in a school you may have fewer students in the sixth form than in other years, and in a representative sample a smaller number of sixth formers would be included. Representative sampling can only be done on those characteristics that are easily identifiable or on which you have previously collected population statistics.

'Quota sampling': this entails identifying subsections of your population which are interesting and taking equal numbers at random from them. So, in the school example, you might be interested in those going to university and those leaving at the end of compulsory schooling. You would take equal numbers from both groups.

Each sampling method has its advantages and disadvantages. The one you choose depends on how far you want to be able to generalise from your data to your entire population. Generally, random sampling or quota sampling are preferred in action research.

The scale of sampling is always a big concern. How many people should you include? Big numbers sound impressive if you want to persuade a policy maker but, if you use a big sample, you will probably only have enough resources (time, money, personnel) to ask each person a few questions. If you go for small samples, you may be able to get more extensive and more intensive data.

There is no golden rule about the size of sample to take. The art is in balancing the size of the sample against the depth of information gathered. Samples can be small as a proportion of your population, if you are dealing with a population that you know is homogeneous (similar to each other on characteristics salient to your research topic). Generalisations based upon a small sample in such cases are likely to be well-founded. Researchers acknowledge that interviewing is time-consuming and costly but produces rich data. They therefore tend to accept smaller absolute sample sizes in interview research. For unstructured or semi-structured interviews an 'achieved sample' of 30–40 would be good – always assuming that your analysis does not then require you to break it down into too many (more than say 5) subsections in order to make comparisons. The number in the sample for structured interviews, which are easier to analyse, would be expected to be greater.

The expression 'achieved sample' brings us to the question of response rates. The achieved sample comprises the people who actually complete the interview (your respondents). Some people may have refused. As a proportion of those you approach, the number who agree to take part must be reasonably high for your conclusions to carry weight. If the response rate is low, you may be basing your conclusions on a biased sample. For instance, in the example of the AIDS/HIV study, it may be that only people who already know a lot about the epidemic are willing to talk to you about it. This would vitiate any conclusions you might draw about the need for no more information to be provided.

One way to increase sample size without making the exercise too costly or too slow is to use group interviewing. Boxes 6 and 7 list the pros and cons and the dos and don'ts of group interviewing.

HOW SHOULD YOU ASK YOUR QUESTIONS?

You will have already specified the research questions for yourself; now they need to be translated into questions that can be put to your respondents. Interviews can use a range of question-and-answer formats which range from the totally structured to the totally unstructured.

CALCULATING A RESPONSE RATE

EXERCISE 6

Response Rates

Knowing the response rate is always necessary. If the response rate is low, anyone can claim that your sample may have been biased. The mere possibility can be enough to discredit your work. Acceptable response rates for large-scale survey research involving interviewing would be anything over 60 per cent. For smaller-scale studies the rates should be higher.

You calculate a response rate by taking the number of those agreeing to be interviewed as a proportion of the number you asked for an interview (expressed as a percentage). So, if you asked 48 and 37 agreed to take part, your response rate would be 77 per cent (calculated by dividing 37 by 48 and multiplying by 100).

What would be the response rate if you asked 345 and 178 agreed?
Answer: 51.6 per cent.

Refusal Rates

The figure normally quoted in research reports is the response rate. Sometimes, however, the refusal rate is used too. This is the percentage of people who actually refused to take part. If you managed to contact all the people on your original sample list, the refusal rate will be whatever is left when you take the response rate from 100 per cent. In the example above it would be 23 per cent. However, very often, you find it is impossible to contact all the people on your list: you have a number of non-obtainables. Non-obtainables are not really refusers and should not, therefore, be included in your refusal rate. So, in calculating your refusal rate, subtract the number who were non-obtainable from the number on your original list, then find out the percentage of the remainder who refused.

Example: What is your refusal rate if your sample list contains 500 names, 140 of these are unobtainable and 50 refuse to take part?
Answer: 13.9 per cent.

Response rates can be given either as a percentage of the total sample list or of those who proved obtainable. Calculate both for the example above.
Answer: For total sample: 62 per cent.
For obtainable sample: 86 per cent.

As you will note, giving response rate against the obtainable sample improves its apparent viability.

GROUP INTERVIEWS:
PROS AND CONS

BOX 6

Group interviewing can be a very valuable research tool. Like all interviewing methods it has advantages and disadvantages.

Advantages

1. You can sample more people at lower cost and greater speed.

2. Groups provide information on how people communicate their ideas. This data is never accessible in one-to-one interviews.

3. Groups discourage habitual or semi-automated responses. Since other group members may challenge an answer, individuals tend to be more analytical and thoughtful.

4. By making diversity of opinion more manifest, groups can stimulate new ideas or promote reconsideration.

5. If change in attitudes or behaviour is the purpose of the research, groups can be useful. It has been known for half a century that discussion groups are very effective in bringing about changes in attitudes and behaviour.

Disadvantages

1. The information collected from any one member of the group will be less.

2. Group interviews are a poor way to explore knowledge: you only learn what the most knowledgeable person in the group knows.

3. Groups are subject to all the usual conformity pressures:
    – dominance by any one person who is very socially-skilled may distort what others are willing to say; so would the presence of a high status participant such as a senior manager or headmaster;
    – fear of losing face will push participants towards giving socially-desirable responses;
    – fear of appearing ignorant will silence some.

4. Bringing together a group of people previously unknown to each other to talk about any serious issue will create an atmosphere of social anxiety.

5. Group interviews share the same interpretation problems that dog all open-ended questioning. They may be exaggerated because the effect of interruptions in the group discussion is to shatter the cohesiveness of an intended statement. Recognising themes in an individual's responses becomes difficult.

GROUP INTERVIEWS: DOS AND DONT'S

BOX 7

The problems of group interviewing are not insoluble as long as the organisation of the session is good. There are guidelines which improve the chances of success:

● 1.　Do not have more than 6 or 7 people in the group. Bigger groups fragment. Do not let sessions last more than 1–2 hours.

● 2.　Expect that some of those who initially agree to partici-pate will fail to turn up, so over-recruit from the start.

● 3.　For most programme evaluation research, you will need to run about 6 groups. If the target population is diverse, you might want to go up to 12 groups.

● 4.　The researcher, or a colleague, acts as the group 'leader' (the label used can be important in establishing a mental set for participants; if you do not wish to be seen as directive, use some other title). Leaders differ in style. Some are very directive, others passive and non-intrusive. The style you adopt depends on the amount of structure you wish to impose. If you have a clear set of questions to be addressed in a set order, it is impossible to be passive. If, however, you want the discussion to flow naturally from one topic to the next, you might wish to intervene only to clarify what is being said or to add a new dimension for them to think about.

● 5.　It is important to have a clear idea of what information you want from the discussion. It is useful to have a topic guide which maps the purpose of the exercise, the ter-ritory you have to cover, your main priorities, and the order in which you would like to get through the topics. The standard topic guide starts with broad, groundclear-ing questions and moves sequentially to more specific details.

● 6. Avoid becoming involved in pre-session chit chat; get the session started with a brief introduction. If you are audio- or video-taping the session, tell them and explain why. Test first to ensure recording is technically good.

● 7. Start with a set of very simple questions so that everyone in the group talks. This might include the standard exercise in self-introduction. If people identify themselves they are more likely to take the session seriously and they are also less likely to reveal sensitive information about themselves.

● 8. Once the participants have settled down, encourage exchanges between group members by becoming more passive. For instance, if you are asked a question, you might reply, 'That's an interesting one. What do you think, Jill?' (addressing someone other than your questioner). Avoid direct questioning: 'What do you mean by that?' A gentler 'Tell us a bit more' is less threatening.

● 9. Never take sides in a dispute. 'Passionate neutrality' is the pose to strike: enthusiasm without bias. Avoid expressing ideas as your own. If you want to support a minority view so that it can be expressed more fully, you can comment that a similar view was expressed in an earlier group.

● 10. Dominant group members have to be prevented from monopolising the discussion. You can do this by pointedly asking for someone else's views; not looking at the dominant speaker; and the deliberate use of impatient body language.

For anyone with experience of therapeutic groups, it is tempting to shift out of the researcher role and into the role of clinical practitioner. This must be avoided.

STRUCTURED INTERVIEWS

Structured interviews involve a fixed set of questions which the researcher asks in a fixed order. Commonly, respondents are expected to choose an answer from a series of alternatives given by the researcher – a type of multiple-choice procedure. Answers can be given against rating scales too. So, for instance, in the example of the AIDS/HIV study, respondents might be asked to say how far they agree or disagree with a series of statements such as:

I worry about the possibility of contracting the virus.
I would read an information sheet on the symptoms of AIDS/HIV.
I know someone with the virus.

This technique is often used by market research companies since it provides information which is easily quantified, it ensures comparability of questions across respondents and makes certain that the main topics are covered. However, it gives little space for new insights. People are not free to give the answers or information which they think important. You may miss a whole area of concern just because you did not think to ask questions about it.

UNSTRUCTURED INTERVIEWS

Unstructured interviews are the opposite. Here the interviewer has a number of topics to cover but the precise questions and their order grow from the exchange with the respondent. Open-ended answers allow people to say as little or as much as they like. Comparability across respondents is sacrificed for personally-relevant information.

Analysis of unstructured interviews is difficult and time-consuming but it would be wrong to think that such data is unquantifiable. The frequency of certain themes, comments, etc., from one person and across a group can be established. There are very sophisticated software packages now (for example, *Ethnograph, Nota Bene*) which will count the incidence of certain phrases or words for you. Others will allow you to use these frequency counts to examine relationships between one characteristic of the sample (say, sex) and another (say, age). However, many people using unstructured interviewing shun all quantification. They argue that their objective is to understand the meaning of what is said and this is not achieved by statistical tests. Rather, it is done through immersing yourself in the data until you think like your respondents, you see the world as they do and, finally, you understand them. This approach, favoured by anthropologists, has great merit. Whether it is persuasive to policy-makers is another matter. Accountants and

planners look for numbers not for what appears on paper to be a sub-jective, and thus challengeable, account by one researcher. On the other hand, interesting quotes taken from unstructured interviews can make a powerful story when strung together properly. For instance, a social worker militating for a new drop-in centre for homeless youths might illustrate the case with quotations which show:
– there is a demand for the centre;
– the role it would serve in the community, not just for young people but for others (that is, its wider value);
– the extent of the distress currently experienced by young people.
Ideally, the quotes would allow your interviewees to speak for them-selves. You act as an editor only in so far as you choose those parts of what they say which are most eloquent and persuasive.

Between these two idealised poles of the structure dimension there are all sorts of compromises. Action research and programme evaluation are usually eclectic, using interviews with questions which are structured in some places, semi-structured in others and totally unstructured elsewhere.

ASKING QUESTIONS

Whether you use structured or semi-structured interviews there are a number of guidelines to follow in drawing up your questions and asking them.

Questions
- *should not be double-barrelled.*
  Example: 'Do you think all homosexuals and drug users should be compulsorily tested for HIV sero-positivity?' A 'No' to this could mean the respondent does not want either homosexuals or drug users tested or could mean that only drug users or only homosex-uals should not be tested.

- *should not assume something before going on to something else.*
  Example: 'Do you think that the vicious attacks on homosexuals appearing in the press have increased since AIDS/HIV was iden-tified?' They may not see the attacks to be vicious in the first place. Again, any answer is uninterpretable.

- *should not include complex or jargon words.*
  Example: 'Sero-positivity' should probably not be used.

- *should not be leading.*
  Example: 'I suppose you know what is meant by the phrase "safer sex"?' Who would say 'No' to that?

- *should not include double negatives.*
  Example: 'Do you think that not many people would not now understand the phrase "safer sex"?' Would you be sure a 'No' meant 'no'?

- *should not require comment on the possibility of hypothetical situations.*
  Example: 'How would you feel if you contracted the virus?' The reliability or validity of any answer would be suspect. Hypothetical questions elicit idealised or socially-desirable responses more often than not.

- *should not act as catchalls.*
  Example: 'Will you tell me everything you have ever heard about the AIDS/HIV epidemic and how it has influenced you?' The most likely result is silence and you will certainly get little comparability across respondents.

▶ **Make yourself thoroughly familiar with the schedule of questions** before you start. Know your route through it (particularly if it differs according to what initial answers you get).

▶ **Ask all questions of all respondents,** even if you think you already know what they will say.

▶ **Decide what each question is meant to tap.** If you are failing to get relevant information probe further. If you have to use probes (i.e. non-committal encouragements to extend answers using eye contact, glance, repeating the answer back to the respondent, mmms and ahhs, gentle queries like 'I'm not quite sure what you mean') make sure that they are non-directive. Prompts (which suggest possible answers to the respondent) can be used but only if they are used consistently for everyone.

▶ **Do not seek or give unrelated or irrelevant information.** Give clarification if asked but again do not be directive.

▶ **Be consistent in recording the answers.** Audio- or video-taping is best because in note-taking translations from the respondent's language or imagery to that of the researcher inevitably occur and can distort the meaning of what has been said.

▶ **Give each respondent an equal hearing.** You will find some respondents that you dislike and disagree with. There is then a tendency to interrupt, hear only what you want to hear, and curtail the interview prematurely. All temptations of this sort have to be ignored. You have to practise appearing comfortable with whatever the respondent says.

▶ **Expect occasional challenges to your authority** and queries about the value of your questions. Unlike the selection or appraisal interview, in the research interview, the balance of power is rarely tipped in favour of the interviewer. You have to negotiate your rights of access to personal or important information. In the research interview conceptions of status are changed: the respondent is the expert in what you want to know.

▶ **Answers in face-to-face interviewing include the non-verbal component as well.** If you only use audio-recording, you might need to note down points where non-verbal communication was strong.

▶ **Avoid encouraging dependency in the respondent** if you are dealing with sensitive subject matter. You have no right to offer advice or counselling unless this has been explicitly agreed with the respondent. If the interview does arouse or upset the respondent it is important not to leave until calmness is restored. If advice is needed, have information ready to give about where it can be obtained after the interview.

Bearing these guidelines in mind, try Exercise 7.

ARTEFACTS AFFECTING THE VALIDITY AND RELIABILITY OF INTERVIEW DATA

The interview approach relies heavily upon respondents being able and willing to give accurate information but there can be motives for lying: respondents may not like the look of the interviewer; they may want to sabotage the research; they may be embarrassed to tell the truth; and so on. Responses may also be affected by lapses of memory of which they are unaware. Getting accurate information on activity patterns even in the near past is notoriously difficult. People simply forget and if they are embarrassed to tell you that, they confabulate.

If you need accurate information on behaviour, you may need to use very careful questioning which carries the respondent sequentially through a day's or a week's activities, with lots of time for backtracking and revision.

You can overcome some of these difficulties by complementing your interview with other data-gathering techniques. For instance, if you are interested in activity patterns, have the respondent fill in an activity diary before coming to the interview. This might include the day broken down into the chunks which interest you and the respondent simply writes down at the end of a morning, or evening, what has been done in each chunk.

Never be afraid to use adjuncts to straightforward questioning. Self-completion questionnaires can be very useful. In sensitive areas of

CREATE AN INTERVIEW SCHEDULE

EXERCISE 7

Work out the schedule of questions which you would ask if you were doing the research in the example concerning AIDS/ HIV. The issue is whether you, as a professional, have responded adequately to the AIDS/HIV crisis. Should you be doing something more to inform the patients/students/clients you work with?

▶ Shape the questions to fit your own working environment. Decide what research questions would be important in your own work context. Decide how structured the questions should be. List them in order. Think about the relationship between them. Do they flow from one another? Cut out inconsistencies. How would you feel about asking them? Have you missed some issues because you would find it embarrassing to ask about them? If the question caused offence, how would you handle it? Who would you refer the respondent to if advice was needed? Where would you do the interview?

▶ What sampling technique would you use? What numbers? What would that tell you? How far could you generalise from the sample?

▶ Try your interview schedule out if you work in a context where you can. The only way to really know if it will work is to try it. All interview schedules should be tried out before you commit yourself to using them. This process of trial and revision is called 'piloting'.

questioning, people are often more willing to disclose information to the unseeing page than to an interviewer.

Validity of information collected is said to improve with repeated interviews. Talking to someone on several occasions seems to increase the sense of rapport and encourages greater commitment and honesty. This may be true, although it has the status of a research community myth rather than an established fact, because it is only those who are committed to the project who will bother to see you several times.

TELEPHONE INTERVIEWING

For many professions, the telephone is the main artery of communication. Forgetting it, when it comes to doing research, may be a mistake. It can be an ideal tool for programme evaluation research because it is cheap and fast. There are a number of points to remember if you decide to do your interviewing by telephone. See Box 8 for guidelines. Remember you can always use telephone interviewing together with other data collection techniques. In repeat interviewing, the switch from face-to-face to the telephone works well.

VALUE OF RESEARCH INTERVIEWING

No method of collecting information is free of faults. This chapter has attempted to present both the strengths and weaknesses of the interview method. When all the problems surrounding question construction, biases introduced by interviewers and respondents, and the limitations of the medium of communication are taken into account, the method still has much to recommend it. It simply has to be used with care and in full acknowledgement of its limitations.

ANALYSING INFORMATION FROM RESEARCH INTERVIEWS

Practitioners using interviewing as a research tool often find that they collect an enormous amount of information and then do not know how to interpret it. The problem is less acute if you use fully-structured interview schedules since response variety is constrained. With unstructured or semi-structured interviews, however, it is sometimes hard to know where to start. There are a few key guidelines to follow which will allow you to proceed.

TELEPHONE INTERVIEWING

BOX 8

Pros

❏ Telephone interviewing seems to achieve similar results. Studies have shown few differences.

❏ Telephone interviewing seems to encourage greater frankness in response to sensitive questions on personal matters (for example, sexual matters). The exception to this is questions about income; money questions are answered reluctantly and with understatement.

❏ Telephone interviewing is cheaper and faster than other methods.

❏ Computer-assisted telephone interviewing (CATI) can be used. The interviewer has a computer which cues the questions to be asked and records the answers ready for analysis. This sort of on-line interviewing is readily available to anyone with access to a PC.

❏ There is no evidence that the vocal qualities of the interviewer affect refusal rates, but more experienced interviewers do have higher success rates.

❏ If you are employing someone else to do your interviewing, it is much easier to monitor the quality of their performance, since they will all be located in the same place and can be overseen.

Cons

❏ By using telephones, you selectively exclude the lower income groups from your sample: about 80 per cent of households have telephones. This does not matter, of course, if your target population is covered.

❏ Response rates are lower (7–20 per cent less than face-to-face interviews). Advance letters, warning that you will call, improve response rates (but not always and not much). Evening and weekend calls and calls to the elderly yield higher refusal rates.

❏ Telephone interviews are more acceptable if they are short (15–20 minutes maximum). If more time is needed, you should book, in advance, a time suitable to the respondent.

❏ Answers on the telephone tend to be truncated in response to open-ended questions. People are faster in their responses; silence is avoided.

❏ Complex questions (or those with a large number of response options) prove more difficult to answer on the telephone. Questions should be structured with this in mind.

▶ Use transcripts of your interviews

If you can afford the time and resources, your first task should be to get audiotapes transcribed so that you have a written record of the interview. Failure to get a transcript can be a false economy because so much information is lost. The record should include indications of pauses, changes of tone, etc., and you can always append the notes which you made of accompanying non-verbal communication (NVC). If you are lucky enough to have video, the description of NVC can be detailed. It can also include any relevant information on your own posture, comments, etc. Transcription is a slow business (7 hours on average for 1 hour taped) so get it started as the interviews happen; do not leave it to the end. Transcriptions will ultimately allow much quicker analysis because they enable you to flick across interviews and back and forth in any one.

If the transcription involves a group interview, make sure you know which person said what. Otherwise you never know whether a thing said frequently was said by only one person or many. It also allows you to look for changes in opinions expressed by any one individual across the interview.

▶ Use experts to help

If you are unsure about how you will analyse your interviews, do not be afraid to ask for advice. Members of social science departments in local universities and colleges will probably help (you may need to offer some recompense but this may be paid in kind, for example, by taking one of their students on placement). If you think you will need such help, seek it at the start of your planning of the interview schedule. Going to them after you have the data can be too late to prevent you spending time on things which subsequently prove unanalysable. You should know enough about interpreting data to know if the advice you are given is not addressing the issues which concern you.

▶ Take advantage of the quantifiability of structured questions

Structured questions which require respondents to choose between alternative answers allow you to make simple statements about how many of what sort of respondent chose each option. Questions that require the respondent to use some rating scale (e.g. 1 to 5 points reflecting extent of agreement) can be used to get average ratings for that item across the whole sample or for some subsections of the sample. People can be profiled in their ratings across a number of questions and compared with the average pattern obtained from the whole sample or with the specific pattern of some other person. Using these simple devices, it is possible to describe clearly what individuals and aggregates of individuals are saying in response to your questions.

▶ **Use your research questions to impose structure after the event**
Where questions are unstructured or semi-structured, you must allow the research questions you specified at the start to act as a prism through which you view the information. Concentrate on those items of information relevant to your research questions. You can use a technique known as content analysis to do this. Essentially, this entails defining a series of categories of answer in which you are interested. Take the AIDS/HIV example: you may have been interested in any occasions when the respondent indicated accurate knowledge of the virus (this would form one category); you may be interested in instances of negative attitudes towards people with AIDS (another category); you might want to note expressions of worry (another category); etc. Having established the categories which interest you, it is possible to look at each interview for the presence or absence of exemplars of that category. This will allow you to say how many people said things fitting into each category. It will also allow you to produce a consistent picture of what each individual had to say on set types of issue.

If you have chosen to use semi-structured or unstructured questions, you may not wish to push responses into categories because this loses some of the individuality of the original statements. If this is so, you might consider using content analysis but supplementing it, in the report you produce of your findings, with lots of quotations which show the depth and diversity of opinion expressed.

There will be problems in determining what categories to use in the content analysis. You are essentially taking a knife and chopping information into chunks. You may have difficulty knowing where to slice. Always be led in these decisions by your research questions. As was mentioned earlier, content analysis can be made faster if appropriate software packages are used. Such software is not, however, the total answer because it will only record what is present.

Some of the best researchers rely on spotting what is absent from an interview in order to draw conclusions. Look for themes which you expect to find in answers but are surprisingly absent. Will this tell you what to do next?

Sometimes people fail to say what is taken for granted, is commonly understood. Ignoring this may be dangerous. Many of the most central understandings in a community are unspoken because no one needs to voice them.

▶ **Your analysis should be open to verification**
You need to give enough information in any description of your work for someone to repeat the analysis. This means that all content analysis categories should be very clearly defined. Often, in using content analysis, a researcher will use someone else who is unaware of the researcher's conclusions to check the interpretation. This necessitates having definitions of the categories which someone else understands and can apply, in the analysis, in an identical way to you. If both analysts come to the same conclusions (which is known as high inter-rater reliability), you can be fairly convinced that the analysis has been conducted rigorously. Of course, it may be that both have consistently made the same mistake, ignoring vital information, but this will be evident to an outsider from the content categories used and the transcripts presented.

▶ **Authenticate your interpretations with your interviewees**
Take your conclusions back to your respondents and find out if they make sense to them. This can both verify your conclusions and open the opportunity to discuss what you intend to do next. After all, action research and programme evaluation are about introducing change. The research shows both where changes are needed and what sort would be acceptable. Before proceeding to introduce changes, you should check that you have made the right inferences.

▶ **Always use all your data**
Data collection is emotionally and financially costly; do not waste any data once you have it. Allow yourself the time to analyse the same data in several ways: different analyses show different facets of the data. You might start with content analysis but then feel that you want to look at the data more holistically, looking for themes, extended lines of rhetoric, etc. Also allow yourself to seek out the correspondences between different types of data you collect. You might have asked questions about different aspects of your respondents' lives. Analysing this aspect by aspect may be interesting but how do they interact? You can always test hypotheses about such relationships even if they were never part of the research plan.

▶ **Keep data**
You never know when you may want it for comparison purposes.

PRESENTATION OF FINDINGS

Following the proforma presented in Exercise 8 will help you to develop ways of presenting your own findings. In writing a report, or in making

REPORTING FINDINGS

EXERCISE 8

Good reports can be as valuable as good research in persuading other people. You should practise writing a report based on the pilot work you did for Exercise 7. If you have some other data set, you can use that. Writing a report for action research or programme evaluation purposes differs somewhat from the standard scientific report. The report should include the following.

1. **Brief summary of your findings,** method of data collection and recommendations for change. The method section of the summary should be very short (for example, 'a series of semi-structured interviews were conducted with a random sample of 58, all involved with my department in some way'). Summaries should be limited to 1 or 2 pages. Most people will only read the summary. It should get your main point across; do not prevaricate.

2. **Description of your objectives** in doing the research: the research questions.

3. **Details of sample,** response rate, and method of data collection used.

4. **Form of analysis used.** Emphasise any steps taken to validate the analysis (for example, second analyst in content analysis, check back with respondents).

5. **Conclusions drawn.** Present these against the backdrop of the actual data. Statistical results should be provided where available. Good graphs and clean tables can replace words. Make it clear that you are aware of any drawbacks in your data or the analysis. Be wary of over-generalisation beyond the population from which the sample is drawn. Make a brief but cogent statement of what you see to be the implications for change. Look at these against current resources and predicted shortfall. Describe any non-obvious advantages in the changes proposed.

The general rule for report writing is parsimony: nothing unnecessary for your argument and its substantiation should be included.

an oral presentation, always remember the nature of your audience and your own objectives in addressing them. Start by showing how what you have to say is relevant to the audience. With audiences that may not initially be interested, present the strong findings first and tell them what changes you would like to see happen.

Research, especially that involving interviewing, takes a lot of effort. Do not waste what you have done either by inadequate analyses or through poor presentation of your findings.

Chapter Seven

Interviews with Children

Children require particularly skilful interviewing. Practitioners are often called upon to conduct interviews with children. Children are the chief concern for teachers, they are a major client group for social services, and they are all too frequent patients for the medical profession and customers for the police. In their dealings with children, practitioners are often seeking information which is needed in the day-to-day pursuit of their work. For instance, from a particular child, a teacher may need to know whether she likes boarding school; from the same child a social worker may need to know whether a step-parent is beating her; and the doctor may want to know what the pain she reports in her tummy feels like and when it started. The information required may be part of the sort of programme evaluation research described in Chapter 6. Whether the information possessed by children is needed for practice or research, it will often be gathered using interviewing.

HAZARDS IN INTERVIEWING CHILDREN

There are a number of hazards which will be encountered if you interview children between the ages of 4 and 10 years. Depending upon the experience and ability of the child, the difficulties may remain after the age of 10.

The tendency to say 'Yes'. Very young children are unwilling to assert themselves and to contradict an adult. They will, therefore, answer questions in any way they think you want them answered. Later, of course, children in the early teenage years may delight in confusing adults, which produces a different problem of interpretation. This means that you have to guard very closely against giving any hint of what you expect them to say. You have to encourage them to disclose their own opinion and this may take many reassurances that you want to know what they think, you want their own ideas, and that there are no right answers. Anything that looks like a test will either silence them or trigger things they know adults want to hear. There is also a strong 'acquiescence response' bias: children will tend to say 'yes', irrespective of the question, if they are anxious to please. So you should try to pose questions which are not open to yes or no responses. For instance, 'Did you like that?', would become, 'What did you think about that?'

The tendency to say 'don't know'. Children will say 'Don't know' for all sorts of reasons:

– they aren't interested in responding
– they don't understand the concepts used in the question
– they don't understand the vocabulary in the question
– they think you expect them not to know
– they don't wish to admit what they know
– they are shy and too embarrassed to say more
– they really do not know.

A 'Don't know' response must be treated cautiously. Never base a conclusion on 'Don't knows', especially one which asserts that children don't know.

Literal interpretations. Young children interpret questions literally. You have to make sure that the questions are clear. For instance, they should not include similes: for example, the answer to 'How do you think James showed that he was as powerful as a lion?' would tell you more about what the child thought about lions than about James.

Distractions. Children pay attention to unexpected details both in the interview context and in the questions. For instance, they may become fascinated by your hair, the fly trapped in the window, or the scabs they can pick on their knees. This can be disconcerting. The only way to retain their attention is to make your interview full of different topics. Use visual prompts (like cartoons or objects); use show cards which illustrate or present questions in a written form for older children; have them act out their answers, etc., in order to change the pace of the interview. Keep the interview short. From small children you would be lucky to get 15 minutes' worth of good questions.

Different priorities. Children have quite different priorities to your own. They might be interested in who you are, if you are new, and they will have their own set of questions to ask you. Do not refuse to answer them but keep the answers short. For the child who gets into the infinite regress of 'Why?', distraction with a new topic is the best strategy. Never lose your temper, show your exasperation, or speak sharply to a child in an interview. In addition to being unprofessional, it is impractical, since children who have been frightened become silent.

Egocentricity. Since young children may have no sense of another person's point of view, always check back with the children that you have understood what they said. If you ask them about why someone behaved towards them in a particular way, they will give you a very egocentric answer. Always check who the children are talking about and the reasons for what they say. For example, you might have asked why a parent punished the child the previous night. The answer might be: 'Because he was angry'. It would be necessary to check whether the child was referring to his own anger or that of his father. Very often children explain what another person does, particularly in relation to themselves, in terms of their own characteristics or behaviour.

Helping them out. There is a great temptation to answer for a child who is hesitating or doubtful; don't.

Distortions. Children are often interviewed in institutional contexts. They are pulled out of the classroom, the dormitory, the hospital ward, to be interviewed individually and are then returned. Once back, they talk to all the other children about the interview. Rumour carries the content of the interview from one child to another very rapidly; it also distorts that content. The result is that children interviewed later may have many misconceptions about what you are doing. This can be established by asking children interviewed later in the series what they have heard about the interview and correcting misunderstandings. Careful explanation of the interview and the reasons for doing it should always be given.

Quiet location. In all interviews, but particularly with children, it is important to avoid locations which are noisy, overlooked, liable to interruptions, not conducive to intimacy or redolent with strong associations (for example, the head teacher's room).

Recording information. Recording what children say at interview can be complex because note-taking is difficult if the respondent has changes of mind, is self-contradictory, or requires lots of encouragement. Children will also question you about the notes you are taking which can be very disruptive. It is best to have someone else in the room taking notes. Otherwise use audiotaping.

Interviewing children is undoubtedly challenging but it can be enlightening and very rewarding. If you are involved in inteviewing them, it is important to consider which of these hazards you can overcome and what the rest mean for the conclusions which you can draw from the information you glean.

Chapter Eight

Media Interviews

Media is the generic term for the press, radio and television. Members of the caring professions are often now targets of media interest; so are other public service practitioners. Some of it is critical: social workers who fail to spot non-accidental injury cases, teachers who fail to keep control in the classroom, or doctors and nurses who strike for extra pay; all are condemned. Some of it is applauding: social work, education and medical staff who keep providing services for the community despite shortages of resources do get praised. The caring professions are particularly attractive targets for media reports because they play a central part in the life of the community; whenever a crisis occurs, the caring professions are at hand to be depicted as heroes or as villains.

WHY BE INTERVIEWED?

The role of the media is to provide information, opinion and entertainment. If you are approached for an interview you should find out how it will be used: to inform, express opinion, or entertain. This shapes the way you approach the interview and, indeed, whether you agree to it. Being approached is both flattering and exciting initially, and can become nerve-racking as the interview proceeds. Your first instinct might be to agree to the interview but you should take time to consider whether it is really in your own interests to do so. You should only agree if you know the way the interview will be used and you feel you genuinely have something to say about the topic. For instance, you might not want to take part if you suspect that you are the 'expert' being pulled in to provide fair game for critics or as intellectual light relief from the heavy business of real entertainment.

Of course, not all interviews are initiated by the media. You may actively want to be interviewed. You may have some information which you want to publicise widely, you may need information or help from the public at large and you may approach the press, radio or TV to ask for an interview. This is a tactic which is becoming more feasible as local radio stations multiply. The media provide a useful tool for a practitioner who wishes to communicate with the community.

MAKING THE BEST OF AN INTERVIEW

Once you have decided that you want to do the interview, you have to make the most of it. There are some general points to remember.

▶ Make sure you are correctly identified.

▶ Get to the venue of the interview early enough to check details and calm down.

▶ Find out the length of the interview; this will tell you how succinct you need to be.

▶ Will you be interviewed alone or with others? If with others, who are they and what position will they take on the issues?

▶ Ask for questions in advance, at least the first two, so that you can plan an answer.

▶ Find out, if you can, which bits of the interview they will use, so that you can comment on editing errors or misrepresentations.

▶ Find out if they intend to juxtapose your inteview with one with somebody who disagrees with you.

▶ Get clearance from your employer, if necessary, to take part.

Over and above these general points, there are some differences of approach needed across the media.

THE PRESS

Two additional things should be remembered about newspaper journalists. First, they are normally working to an editorial brief and have an angle they want to push. Their questions will reflect this line. If it is not one you support, you may need explicitly to discuss it and re-negotiate the way you are willing to be interviewed. Second, you may

MAKE A MEDIA MESSAGE

EXERCISE 9

Imagine you are approached by the local newspaper to give an account of your work in 100 words. What would you say to the reporter?

After you have written your 100-word response, rate it on a scale from 1 to 5 (1 = very poor, 2 = quite poor, 3 = uncertain, 4 = quite good, 5 = very good) on the following characteristics:

? Intelligible to the average reader.
? Free of jargon that is not explained.
? Informative about your work.
? Covers the important things which you do.
? Interesting to the average reader.
? Useful to the average reader.

You may find that producing something which gets high ratings on all six characteristics takes several attempts. Anything which rates badly on all these characteristics will do you more harm than good. All publicity is not good publicity.

Before you agreed to give your description to the reporter, you would, of course, need to know why the request was being made and the context in which your answer would appear. The answers to these two questions would shape what you produced. If the newspaper's intention was critical, you might want to forestall it either by refusal to cooperate or by structuring your answer very carefully. Show your final version to someone who knows your work and ask this person to rate it on the characteristics above. Look for differences in the way you perceive your message and the way your friend does. Discuss improvements that could be made.

want to respond 'off-the-record'. This is a recognised practice: information is not ascribed to the source.

This can obviously be used to 'leak' information. It can also be used more ordinarily where the information you provide is commonly available in your profession, there is no reason for secrecy, but you simply do not wish to have public attention focused upon you.

TELEVISION

You can use the guidelines from Exercise 9 in generating all media messages, including those for TV interviews.

▶ **Say it simply.**

▶ **Make it informative.**

▶ **Keep it useful.**

Television studios with the cameras, lights, microphones and technicians besides the interviewer, other guests and, probably, an audience are awe-inspiring. Concentrate on the interviewer (and the other interviewees, if there are some), and ignore the rest. Do not look into the camera or make remarks directly to the audience.

Dress so that you are comfortable. Choose clothes which will relax you in the heat of the studio. Pick ones which are not garish or visually disruptive. You can use your clothes to make a statement if you want. Just be sure you know what they are saying.

You will probably be taken into make-up before the interview. It is best not to make up heavily yourself beforehand. The time in the make-up chair can be very relaxing; you are in the hands of highly professional people. Treat it as a time to calm yourself. However, if you do not want make-up, you do not have to have it.

With modern cameras and editing facilities, you do not have to sit very still in order to stay in shot. Relax, wave your arms if you need them to make a point. Rely upon the professionalism of the TV director and technicians to frame the picture. Your task is to be interesting while you persuade or inform.

You cannot expect to be able to use notes in a television interview. Prepared answers have to be memorised. It is best just to memorise the main points you want to make and then ad lib. Never underestimate either the basic ignorance of your interviewers or their general intelligence and skill. It is a lethal combination because it pushes you towards offering over-simplified explanations which can then be torn apart. The note to aim for is the explanation you would offer someone who is your peer but from another professional group.

If you are one of a number of interviewees, you may have to abandon your originally intended response anyhow in order to react to something someone else has just said. It is essential to listen to what other interviewees are saying, even if you then deliberately ignore it.

If you are part of a panel of interviewees, you may find it difficult to get a word in edgeways. If you fail to catch the presenter's eye, you should use his or her name in starting your intervention: for instance, 'Terry, I know that . . . ' or 'Sue, you can always tell . . . '. Naming attracts attention. The other way to do it is to come straight into the flow of the conversation with an agreement with what someone has just said: for example, 'I agree with Paul that . . . '. Then say what you really wanted to say which may have nothing to do with Paul's point. Never try to intervene with a phrase starting with 'but', 'perhaps', or anything else indefinite. Powertalk again can come into play here.

RADIO

Radio has the advantage of making you invisible. Your voice and your words take on new significance. They make pictures unadulterated by feature or appearance. Radio, therefore, requires greater precision in the statements you make. The compensation is that you can take notes into the studio and you can make notes during the interview.

The same rules about answers which lace simplicity with sophistication apply as in TV or press interviews. The main problem with radio is that there is a pressure to avoid silence; you feel the need to answer quickly, in contrast to TV, where you might pause and look thoughtful before speaking. This can result in convoluted sentence structures. You say what you mean but it comes across as very complex. A second's reflection before you spoke would have reordered the presentation of ideas to make them more accessible. Do not stall completely, but do take your time before answering, using some stock filler like, 'That's an interesting issue' if you really do abhor the silence.

Members of the caring professions in particular tend to be increasingly involved in phone-in programmes. These can be the ultimate trap since there is no way to predict questions and callers may ask some very strange things. A good presenter will protect you from the worst excesses of the audience but you have to know when to say 'I do not know what you mean' or 'I really cannot answer that' or 'I disagree with you because . . . '. If you do decide to take part in a phone-in, you need to have clear objectives in mind. If there are particular messages you want to transmit, you need to be persistent and consistent throughout the programme.

MEDIA INTERVIEWS BY TELEPHONE

EXERCISE 10

Imagine that you are at work, an average day, and the telephone rings. Without warning you are asked whether you have time to answer a few questions for a researcher working for a national television company collecting background information for a story to be aired later in the day. The questions concern a topic with which you are very familiar.

How would you respond? What questions would you need to ask before you were willing to answer those of the researcher? What precautions would you take to ensure the caller was actually bona fide? What would you need to do to clear any statements you might make with your employer? It is good to have a standard technique ready for telephone contacts of this sort.

▶ Get a clear picture of who they work for. 'Cold contact' by telephone is often used by freelance researchers/reporters who are doing a story speculatively in the hope of getting someone to take it. You can waste a lot of time talking to them for pieces which never appear.
▶ Check they are really working where they say by 'phoning back and checking with the switchboard.
▶ Establish what their hook, angle or line will be in their story. You might not wish to be associated with it.
▶ Insist on having a list of all their questions in advance. Then prepare your answers and ring back. If you have to do any serious preparation, calculate the time and state the fee. Established companies will often agree to payment.
▶ In constructing your answers don't assume any background knowledge. Start from basics and work up. Good journalists ask questions which give the impression of knowledge because they require knowledge to answer them.
▶ If need be, clear your answers with your employer.
▶ Do not be led into over-statement or greater disclosure than you intended. The telephone interview creates a false sense of intimacy.
▶ Do not be led by subsequent questions to talk about issues that you have had no time to think about. Where leading questions are taboo in social research, they are common in media interviews.
▶ Find out whether you will have a chance to check the broadcast before it goes out – you might be able to correct any misrepresentation of your position which has crept in accidentally during editing.

TAKING AN ACTIVE PART

It is actually time that the health professions, teachers and social and public service personnel started to take a more active part in the media. There is no reason why more practitioners should not turn the tables and step onto the other side of the media interview table. It would be good to see practitioners becoming media interviewers. This might be one way to put to good use all of the interview skills described in this book. It would certainly make it possible to lay to rest some of the hero and villain myths which imbue current media representations of teachers, social workers and medical practitioners.

References

Cronbach, L.J. (1984) *Essentials of Psychological Testing 4th ed.* New York: Harper and Row.
Edelmann, R. (1987) *The Psychology of Embarrassment* Chichester: Wiley.
Fontana, D. (1989) *Managing Stress* London: British Psychological Society/Routledge.
Glick, P., Zion, C., and Nelson, C. (1988) What mediates sex discrimination in hiring decisions? *Journal of Personality and Social Psychology, 55* (2), 178–186.
Orpen, C. (1984) Attitude similarity, attraction, and decision-making in the employment interview. *The Journal of Psychology, 117,* 111–120.
Smith, M. and Robertson, I. (Eds) (1989) *Advances in Selection and Assessment* Chichester: Wiley.

Further Reading

British Psychological Society Standing Press Committee (1989) *Media Handbook.* Leicester: British Psychological Society.
Brenner, M., Brown, J., and Canter, D. (Eds) (1985) *The Research Interview: Uses and Approaches.* London: Academic Press.
Goodworth, C.T. (1979) *Effective Interviewing for Employment Selection.* London: Business Books.
Mucchielli, R. (1986) *Face to Face in the Counselling Interview.* London: Macmillan.
Powney, J. and Watts, M. (Eds) (1987) *Interviewing in Educational Research.* London: Routledge & Kegan Paul.
Roberts, C. (1985) *The Interview Game and How It's Played.* London: BBC Publications.
Sykes, W. and Hoinville, G. (1985) *Telephone Interviewing on a Survey of Social Attitudes.* London: Social and Community Planning Research.
Turner, C.T. and Martin, E. (1985) *Surveying Subjective Phenomena (Vols 1 & 2).* New York: Russell Sage Foundation.
Walker, R. (Ed.) (1985) *Applied Qualitative Research.* Aldershot, Hants: Gower.

Index

ACQUIESCENCE, response in children 91
advertising 8, 24, 29, 30
    strategies 34
aggression 32
    of interviewers 55
analysis
    of changes 62
    of information 9
    of job (job analysis) 23–24, 34, 66
    of research interviews 85
anxiety 35, 40–41, 46
    overcoming anxiety 48
    social anxiety 75
application forms 14, 24, 32, 46
appraisal questionnaire 63, 66
assertiveness 32, 47
assessment
    centres 55–56
    interviews 58–60
    tasks 56–58
    techniques 6
attention span 11
    in children 91
attitudes
    of interviewee 11
    to job 19
    similarity of 32
audio-taping 77, 80, 81, 93
    transcripts of 85

BIAS 15, 24, 25, 27–31, 32, 33, 34, 35, 44, 46,
    47, 54, 56, 91
body language
    see non-verbal communication
boredom 19, 23, 40, 52
briefing
    interviewers 14
    interviewees 15
    sessions 29, 56

CAREER, plan 42
    timetable 65
communication skills 27, 28, 56, 59
comparability 45, 78, 80
computer
    records 68
    software 78, 86
    assisted telephone interviews (CATI) 84
conflict 19, 55
consistency 40
    of responses 54
    with self image 55

content analysis 86–87
creative thinking 56
curriculum vitae 14

DATA COLLECTION TECHNIQUES 81
decision making 52–54
disclosure
    self disclosure 13, 19, 40, 41, 47
    self disclosure in children 91
    unexpected disclosure 9
dominant group members 75, 77
dress 33, 46, 97

EGOCENTRICITY 92
emotional responses 43
enthusiasm 31
evaluation
    in appraisal interviews 66–67
    programmes 7
    programme research 76
expectations
    of candidate 59
    of interviewers 54
    of organisation 61
eye contact 37, 42
    see non-verbal communication

FACIAL EXPRESSION 42
fear 41
feasibility analysis 64
feedback 7, 9, 12, 16, 20, 36, 49, 67, 68
filtering
    of applicants 30
flexibility 43, 52, 61

GAME PLAYING 27
goals 63, 68
group discussions 27, 75, 77
    transcriptions of 85

HIDDEN AGENDA 30
honesty 11, 31, 47, 68, 69, 83
humour 31, 42, 47, 55
hypothetical
    interviews 31
    questions 80

INDIRECT QUESTIONS 17
individual differences 31, 58
information
    giving 11
    medical 14

interactions 9
  active 8
  passive 8
internal appointments 44–45
  candidates 45, 54
interview schedules 83, 85
interviewer differences 31, 59
introductory questions 35

JARGON 36, 79, 96
job analysis 23–24, 34, 66
job descriptions 11, 17, 18, 23–24, 30
job satisfaction 11
journalists 95

LEADERSHIP 59, 76
leading questions 41, 79, 99
legislation 68
  legal restraints 13, 16
leisure activities 31, 34
local radio 24, 95
lying 42, 58, 81

MANAGEMENT BY OBJECTIVE 6, 7, 61, 63, 68
marginal candidates 6
media misrepresentation 99
medical information 14
misunderstandings 37, 43
  in children 92
motivation 66
multiple choice procedure 78

NEGOTIATION 6, 22
nervousness 11
non-verbal communication 37, 42–43, 77, 81, 85
note-taking 39, 80, 93, 97, 98

OBJECTIVES 6, 10, 22, 45, 46, 61–66, 68
  management by 6, 7, 61, 63, 68
  objective criteria 34
  objective indices 33
observation
  of interviewees 56
  of interviews 31
off-the-record information 97
open-ended
  answers 78
  questions 75, 84
oral presentations 89

PATH ANALYSIS 31
pedigree 27, 29, 34
performance
  evaluation of 61–62
  indicators 6, 7, 61–67

self-evaluation 63
personal questions 37
personality assessment 39
  (see psychometric tests)
phone-in programmes 98
physical attractiveness (of applicants)
  31, 32, 34, 46
piloting 82
planning exercises 27
posture 37, 42
  see non-verbal communication
powertalk 47, 98
predictability of responses 42
prejudice 12, 13, 16, 60
preliminary interviews 21
preparation 9
  for appraisal 63
presentation of self 18, 46
prestige
  connections 47
  networks 33
probes 80
productivity 28, 29, 34
programme evaluation research 83
promotion 44–45
  decisions 35
  prospects 17
prompts 80
psychometric tests 6, 27, 38, 39

QUALIFICATIONS 14, 17, 24, 46, 49
questionnaires
  appraisal 63, 66
  personality 39
  self-completion 81
questions
  hypothetical 80
  indirect 17
  introductory 35
  leading 41, 79, 99
  open-ended 75, 84
  personal 37

RADIO 95
  interviews 98
rating scales 78, 85
recall of information 20, 39
recording of information 9, 15, 20, 35, 39
referees 24, 26
  reports 43
references 45
refusal rates 74, 84
relaxation 48
reliability
  inter-rater reliability 87
  of assessments 59

of interview data 81
of psychometric tests 38
repeat interviews 7, 83
report writing 88–89
response rates 73–74, 84
rewards and punishments 62, 64, 66–67
rights
    of access to information 81
    of interviewer 8

SAMPLING METHODS 72–73
    population 72
    quota 72
    random 72
    representative 72
    size of sample 73
schedule of questions 44, 45, 52, 59, 80
selection
    criteria 24–26, 37, 39, 41, 44, 49, 50, 52, 59
    procedure 37, 38, 51
    process 34, 35
self-
    assessment 3, 13, 62
    doubt 48
    disclosure 13, 19, 40, 41, 47, 91
    evaluation 63
    interest 18
    presentation 18, 46, 47, 54
    report 26
semi-structured interviews 73
    analysis of 83
sensitive issues 8, 27, 37, 81, 84
sex differences 31, 32, 45, 47
sex-typing of job 32, 33
shortlisting 6, 12, 14, 15, 52

show cards 91
similarity of attitudes 32
speech patterns 32, 37
statistics
    statistical approaches 31
    statistical results 88
stereotypes 3, 30, 33, 46
stereotyping 47
stress 55
    see anxiety
structured interviews 78
    analysis of 83

TECHNIQUES for data collection 81
television 95
    interviews 97–98
training
    of interviewers 59–60
    for interviewees 68
transcripts 85, 86

UNRELIABILITY 59
    see reliability
unstructured interviews 73, 78–79
    analysis of 83

VALIDITY, of assessment techniques 58
    of information 35, 42, 81, 83
    of psychometric tests
video-taped interviews 59, 80
    discussion groups 77
    transcripts 85
voting 53–54

WORK ENVIRONMENT 6, 11, 12, 13, 14